CHINOOK
CREW 'CHICK'

This book is dedicated to my dad, who hates to fly but loves to write.

*And to my mum, for bearing the brunt of my PTSD
and still loving me.*

CHINOOK
CREW 'CHICK'

HIGHS AND LOWS OF FORCES LIFE FROM THE LONGEST SERVING FEMALE RAF CHINOOK FORCE CREW MEMBER

LIZ McCONAGHY

AIR WORLD

AIR WORLD

CHINOOK CREW 'CHICK'
Highs and Lows of Forces Life from the Longest Serving
Female RAF Chinook Force Crew Member

First published in Great Britain in 2022 by
Air World
An imprint of
Pen & Sword Books Ltd
Yorkshire – Philadelphia

ISBN 978 1 39907 292 2

Typeset by SJmagic DESIGN SERVICES, India.

Printed and bound in the UK by CPI Group (UK) Ltd.

Pen & Sword Books Limited incorporates the imprints of Atlas, Archaeology, Aviation, Discovery, Family History, Fiction, History, Maritime, Military, Military Classics, Politics, Select, Transport, True Crime, Air World, Frontline Publishing, Leo Cooper, Remember When, Seaforth Publishing, The Praetorian Press, Wharncliffe Local History, Wharncliffe Transport, Wharncliffe True Crime and White Owl.

For a complete list of Pen & Sword titles please contact

PEN & SWORD BOOKS LIMITED
47 Church Street, Barnsley, South Yorkshire, S70 2AS, England
E-mail: enquiries@pen-and-sword.co.uk
Website: www.pen-and-sword.co.uk

Or
PEN AND SWORD BOOKS
1950 Lawrence Rd, Havertown, PA 19083, USA
E-mail: Uspen-and-sword@casematepublishers.com
Website: www.penandswordbooks.com

MIX
Paper from
responsible sources
FSC® C013604

Contents

Chapter 1

That Guy on the Rope …

'She's awake' … these are the words I hear as my eyes bang open and I realise I'm still alive … this is the moment I have my second chance at life; this is the moment that inspired me to write my story.

My earliest childhood memory as a kid was at Christmas aged about 4 or 5. I grew up in Northern Ireland where it seemed fairly commonplace to have a 'good room'. This was a room purely for special occasions such as posh visitors or Christmas Day. The rest of the year was spent in the 'actual' living room with the TV and scattered Lego boxes everywhere. Now don't get me wrong, our family was definitely not rich or posh in any way, but we had the luxury of space as we lived way out in the countryside of Newtownards up near Scrabo Tower, a feature that stands proud on the hill overlooking the town. No matter where in the world my travels have taken me, as soon as I see Scrabo Tower I know I'm home. My dad had built our house from scratch; he was not a builder by trade but a bike mechanic and owned the local bike shop named after him: 'Mike the Bike'. On Christmas Eve, my older brother and I would put out our pillowcases on the armchairs in the 'good room'; no posh stockings just simple pillowcases. Mine was always on the chair next to the Christmas tree and his was the one near the door. The 'good room' sofa set was a ghastly shade of orange, but this was trendy back in the mid-1980s – at least that's what my mum says now when I still ridicule it. On Christmas morning, Graham (who was two years older than me) and I pushed the door open to be greeted by our chairs awash with goodies and pillowcases overflowing. Santa didn't wrap pressies in our house as he was 'too busy', so we could instantly see what he had delivered. I dashed past my brother's chair this particular morning and noticed it was laden with army clobber. A camouflage jumpsuit, hat, toy guns etc., etc. ... and mine was covered in all things pink. A pink plastic ironing board instantly drew my attention, but then as I perused my chair in amongst all the lovely pink toys, next to the pink plastic iron (that matched the pink ironing board) and the pink dressing gown was a combat-coloured, camouflage-patterned hat. It instantly stood out as it made my plethora of pink look messy. I picked it up, walked over to my brother's chair and set the ugly hat on it. My mum retrieved it, while I continued to open my pressies, and repositioned it on my chair. Nope, Santa must have put this on the wrong chair I informed her as I trotted with it across to Graham's chair again. I noticed he had a similar style hat in olive green on his chair as I placed it down again. Mum then picked it off his chair once more and said, 'Maybe Santa wanted you to have one as well so you can play "Army" with your brother.' I think for the next three years that hat never left my head.

We had a great childhood. Dad built us a tree hut in the overgrown bank that surrounded our garden, and we spent hours playing combat in the woods opposite the house. We were also so lucky to have a neighbour up the road who was the same age and lived on a farm. We would leave the house in the morning and head off with a packet of Tayto crisps and buttered white bread to make crisp sandwiches, along with a Wagon Wheel in our little rucksacks. It sounds like a ridiculously dreamy childhood, and truth be told it was. In those days you could send your kids off for hours on end to fall out of trees and scratch their legs on nettles and twigs and they would still come home safe and sound before dark. I look back now and feel so privileged to have had the most amazing childhood and that my parents gave us the freedom to roam. Eventually, despite being such a tomboy growing up, upon reaching secondary school I discovered dresses and high heels and this lust for combat clothes and games most certainly wore off. So much so that I didn't even join one of Northern Ireland's biggest cadet forces at Regent House, my grammar school. Nope – hockey sticks, high heels and handbags were now my main focus, along with Boyzone and the school rugby team.

I'd once said to my mum that when I grew up, I wanted to be a stripper – no I really did as I arrived into the kitchen aged 7 wearing her burgundy nightie with a belt around my waist and her far-too-big high heels. But after the age of 8 when that phase wore off, I said I wanted a job that if I was asked on a gameshow what I did, people would be 'oh what's that job about?' rather than a lawyer, doctor, banker etc. Joining the forces was never an option I considered at all, because going to university and gaining a degree was unanimously pressed upon us by our school as the only viable pathway to a successful career. Even if it was in 'underwater basket weaving', a degree was essential to making anything of your life. Thankfully, my parents didn't necessarily agree and just wanted us to be proud of what we did for a career and, most importantly, to be happy. My older brother was a super science boffin at school but broke his collarbone in a BMX bike accident during his A levels so decided to revisit his childhood days and join the army rather than pursue a career in maths or science. I think at the time my father was slightly disappointed with his choice but now looks at him in awe of what an amazing choice he made and the outstanding career it led to as REME aircraft engineer. I went with him to Palace Barracks on the day of his entrance test, and this was when I first discovered the job role that would define my entire existence. Sitting in the waiting area, aged 16, I picked up a magazine that had a man hanging out of the side of a helicopter on the cover. I asked the chap behind the desk what this 'guy on the rope's job was called'. He corrected me by telling me it was in fact a wire, and that the job title was Helicopter Crewman or RAF loadmaster as a trade. Instantly I wanted to become that. I didn't really understand what 'that' was, but I wanted to be it!

Now coming back to my school persona, I was one of those annoyingly positive, team corralling types. I was captain of the hockey team, which was my life, and nominated as a prefect. Don't be fooled, I was not that little miss good-looking, popular gal. I always danced around the periphery of the 'cool girls' gang but the fact that my parents owned a holiday caravan, and I didn't smoke meant I was never quite A-list. I almost became 'cool gang essential' when I passed my driving test and was able to take my mates out for lunch in my little green Corsa. This, however, was short-lived. I spilt milk in it unbeknownst to me at the time, and this resulted in my little car smelling as though I had a dead granny locked up in the boot for the whole summer. We used to head out to the car park five minutes early, I would open all the doors, let the smell dissipate to a non-toxic level then we would climb in. We must have looked hilarious as we hung our heads out of the open windows for the five-minute transit up to town. Definitely not looking the coolest in my wheels. None of this was helped by my woeful choice aged 17 to ask my hairdresser to cut my beautiful long hair to give me a Victoria Beckham 'pixie cut'. The result ended with me resembling an angry lesbian, which coupled with the fact that I was, shall we say 'rotund', meant I was also never a decent catch to any of the boys' gang either! But because of these insecurities I did in fact develop a decent sense of humour and was always described as the 'fun one', we all know what that's code for … and I was a huge team player as I always wanted to be loved and included. I was very gregarious and just loved people and making them happy. This makes a lot of sense looking back now as to how some of my life choices came about.

In September 2000, aged 18, my new power suit on (which complemented my lesbian hair cut a treat) I headed up to Palace Barracks for my own initial interview to join the RAF. As I arrived and pulled into the layby to get my car pass from the guard room, a huge helicopter came right over the top of my little green car and landed. I'm sure this was a sign looking back, as this aircraft, the mighty Chinook helicopter was to become the platform on which I would spend my entire seventeen years of military life. I passed my initial interview that day and was scheduled to head to RAF Cranwell a few weeks later for Officer and Airmen Selection College. This in itself was a big deal as I had only ever left Northern Ireland once before and was such a country bumpkin. If I tell you that I thought Leeds was near London that may indicate just how naïve and unaware I was.

On the morning of my flight to Heathrow, I was driving up the only stretch of motorway north of Belfast when, without warning, the bearings collapsed in my somewhat 'cursed' car's wheel. This sent me into a series of 360-degree turns bashing into the middle barrier and ending with me sitting on the hard shoulder facing the right way. It was fifteen seconds of sheer fear and carnage, demolishing the front of the car, but thank God the road was empty when it happened, or I honestly think someone would have been killed. The downside of that of course, is that when traffic did now zoom past it looked to all intents and purposes as if I had just pulled over nice and neatly into the hard shoulder, so no one stopped to help. My parents were on holiday at the time, but I managed to call the emergency services from one of those motorway phones and the police were there in minutes. On asking where I was headed, I explained that I had to get to the airport as I had to fly to England, as I had to get to RAF Cranwell as I HAD to join the RAF. They put me in their car, blues and twos on and whisked me up to Aldergrove in time for me to catch my flight. The lovely female officer felt so sorry for me she even walked me in to get checked in. A fact that I now realise made me look like a convicted criminal.

Sitting on the Underground (actually on the floor of the carriage) for the first time in my life later that morning as I crossed from Heathrow to Kings Cross, I burst into tears. The shock of what had happened a few hours earlier had finally caught up with me. I may as well have peed myself in the corner though as no one wanted to know or ask me if I was OK. Do not look at the crying teenager, whatever you do avoid eye contact. Finally, I pulled myself together and made it to RAF Cranwell. First, we had aptitude tests to complete. These you cannot practise improving, you either have aptitude or you don't. They range from remembering sequences of numbers to reaction tests, such as 'screen turns blue press the blue button'. There were also some pilot-orientated hand-eye co-ordination tests such as 'keep the ball in the middle' or 'hold the line on the horizon'. Amazingly, I did OK in these and actually made the grade for Navigator, but following my medical assessment was told my arms were 2cm too short. It was irrelevant really as even if I had made the grade to be the first direct entrant to the Red Arrows, I still only ever wanted to be a crewman. Next was a medical. This offered some light relief to an otherwise tense day. The chap who was in line before me had been chatting casually before being called in by the nurse. He reappeared twenty minutes later looking rather sheepish. 'Well, that was awful,' he said. I instantly asked why as my heart began to pound with nerves, what did he mean, what would I have to do? 'Well,' he said, 'the nurse asked me to strip to the waist, so I did while she had her back to me but got the wrong end of the stick.' She had meant from the neck down, not the feet up and Lee was now sitting there in his shirt, jacket and tie with nothing else on below.

We also had a series of little problem-solving exercises to carry out, such as 'cross an imaginary pit of molten lava, using three buckets and a plank of wood'. This again went well, and we took it in turn to play the leader. I also passed my fitness test, which was a miracle, considering a month beforehand I could barely run a mile. Yes, I was in the hockey team as I mentioned but I was the position of 'sweeper', a cleverly allocated position in front of the goalkeeper for those whose running ability is, shall we say, somewhat slower. But I made a good wide block as a last line of defence. What I realised that day though is that when you want something badly enough your body can do amazing things. You can push it much further than you expect. This lesson is one I have carried with me forever.

But last was my interview, the most daunting bit. A panel of high-ranking RAF officers asking me current affairs questions and the usual stuff to decipher how much I knew about the RAF. The answer to this was, barely anything. I had read lots of information before the interview, but I was still a young naïve little girl from the countryside in Co. Down. I think I answered three questions correctly by the end and kept blurting out answers to previous questions when the answer suddenly sprang to mind. Hardly a polished interview technique. What they did ask, however, was how my journey to come over to the interview had been, maybe as a way of settling me as I was so clearly out of my depth. I recounted the story of the car crash that morning and getting myself to the airport in a police car and through the Underground for the first time etc. If they had a box on their tick sheet in front of them saying 'tenacious' they must have ticked it instantly. I often wonder if it was that question and my harrowingly honest rapid-fire answer that got me into the RAF that day. Maybe that or they had another few diversity boxes to tick, Irish, blonde, slightly overweight and a lesbian, tick. I'm not an ACTUAL lesbian by the way just to clear that up for any potential male suitors reading, don't put the book down just yet. Anyhow, somehow, I passed the interview and was offered a place on course No. 209 Aircrew Selection Training that September. Yikes ... My world was about to expand exponentially from the 20-mile radius bubble that I lived in.

I continued to see out my A levels: Biology, Geography and Geology, which I had only picked for the field trips. But truth be told I wasted them as I knew I had now been accepted into the RAF and the idea of a fall-back plan didn't even register. I wish I had worked harder at them looking back, not for the grades but for the knowledge retention. I have seen some amazing countries since then and having in-depth geology recall at my fingertips could have made me sound well-smart! I handed in my notice at my part-time job in the local leisure centre café. Incidentally, this was another reason I was slighter softer round the edges. I loved this little part-time job as all my mates worked there too, but I ate most of the profits! The day of my last shift, I set off from home to drive the ten minutes to work, and on walking in the phone rang in the servery area. Margret passed me the hand set and said, 'It's your mum Liz.' What had I forgotten? was my first thought. 'Put on the TV in the café,' she said, 'you need to see a TV now Elizabeth.' Knowing by her tone something serious had happened, we all made our way to the kids' play corner to turn on the TV, just as the second plane flew into tower two. None of us could believe our eyes and what was unfolding in front of them. As we watched in horror, Margret elbowed me and said, 'You're joining the military next week, you will be busy.' And it dawned on me she may be right, and she absolutely was. The events of 9/11 would shape the future of my time in the forces, and actually for the better, but I just didn't know it yet …

That week, America declared their war on terror in Afghanistan where the Taliban had been sheltering Osama Bin Laden who was responsible for the twin towers' attacks. Where the Yanks go, the British Forces follow and shortly the entire British Forces deployed On Operations in support of the United States. If that event hadn't happened, I still think my entire life in the RAF would have been a lot less exciting than the one I was about to begin.

Chapter 2

Fat Lass at the Back

So, on Sunday, 23 September 2001, with a hangover from my leaving party in the local pub in Newtownards, I began the journey over to Cranwell. Thankfully, this time it was much slicker, as I now had a few large bags in tow. These contained some of the kit I had already been issued, such as my boots that I had been given to break in, along with the clothes and some luxuries to get me through the next twelve weeks. Unfortunately, this inventory consisted of forty-eight wooden coat hangers, two pairs of jeans and three tops, and of course 'that' power suit and matching flat, lesbian shoes. My mother had read the joining instructions that the RAF had sent through, which stated that 'wooden coat hangers would be essential'. She was so concerned that I wouldn't be able to get any in England she packed me off with an entire suitcase full of them. Thankfully, I was spared other essentials that you can't buy in England such as jam, potatoes, and cheese and onion Tayto crisps. This is the point I wish I could put an emoji in my book, displaying my sheer disbelief.

I arrived at Grantham station and was met by the RAF driver sent to meet us. Any new recruits stood out a mile, all fresh-faced and wide-eyed, usually looking lost. We were scooped up and led on to the bus which would deliver us to the very front door of the barrack block that would become home for the duration of the course. What an exceptional service, I hear you cry. Looking back, it was most probably done this way so that we wouldn't get lost wandering around camp as every building looked identical. Having now spent seventeen years serving, I realise that this service was a one-off in terms of efficiency when it comes to the RAF MT (Motor Transport) section. Maybe it was another way of reassuring any last-minute doubters that they were joining an 'excellent' organisation. Climbing off the bus, we were met by a few lads in uniform who I assumed were the staff helping us unload our bags from the luggage compartment below the bus and into our block. It didn't take long for them to realise I had mistaken them for staff and while laughing explained that they were the 're course-ees' from the previous intake and were actually now our fellow course mates. There was also one gent, not a 're course-ee' but slightly mature in years compared to most of us youngsters, who really seemed to know his stuff.

This was Dave Grohl, or Grohly as he introduced himself. I will mention now that nearly all military people adopt a nickname, either from a moment of poor judgement in their history or if not then simply by adding a 'y' on to their surname. Grohly was already a serving member of the RAF regiment, and despite initially appearing a little scary as he knew so much, he was straight in with a little 'Norn-Irish' banter and just as helpful as could be. Turns out we had met before during one of the initial interview stages. Clearly, I was so nervous I remember nobody, but Grohly regaled a lovely story of the image I had left him with. Little chunky Norn-Irish girl with a black skirt suit on and massive white pants on show. This also, is another emoji moment. Thankfully, due to Grohly's epic fashion sense, this was the last fashion 'faux pas' I think I ever made. From that day on, Dave became my muse. He held duties ranging from best mate, father figure, uncle, big brother and 'bridesman' when I eventually got hitched fifteen years later. He still to this day remains my 'go to' confidant for guidance on life, rock music and style.

I must admit the only thing I can recall from that first week of basic training was the Monday when we attested. This is the monumental moment when you swear an oath to serve Queen and Country. Everything else that week was a blur. We were given copious amounts of paperwork to sign, we were marched down to stores to get the rest of our kit, and we were introduced to all the Directing Staff, or DS for short. We had lessons on ranks and who to salute and what the rank slides meant. Luckily for me I had joined the service that rather helpfully just added a little extra line to the rank slide each time you were promoted. I remember thinking at the time this is the most ridiculous system and just could not get my head around it. In summary: lots of lines, big wig and salute a LOT; just one line, baby officer but still salute. Every rank in between was best guess to me, and I did indeed spend the first month running around Cranwell saluting anything that moved, including the corporal at the main gate.

By the second week things had gathered pace. Our days began with an inspection every morning, standing at the end of our bed space. We didn't have individual rooms just a space with our bed, a sink, and a wardrobe; a wall separating us from the next occupant. This may sound harsh but honestly the camaraderie and laughs we had. I think nowadays the recruits may get the privacy of their own rooms. This would have been a disaster for me as I learnt so much by the gregarious nature of this accommodation and through osmosis of the two other females on my course. One of whom was Emma, who was also already serving as a chef; the other Kate, an outward bounds instructor. They both had so much more life experience than me and took me under their wing in our three little bed spaces at the end of 'A' wing. We became experts in folding our 'bed packs' – which is basically a funny rectangle sandwich of sheets and scratchy woolly blankets – and had almost individual pride at how neat we could make our 'hospital' corners where you folded your bedsheet over the sides of the horrible green rubber mattress. I remember one particular morning sleeping on the floor beside my bed, then getting up at 5 a.m. to iron, yes iron, my bed that was already made up! And obviously my pride and joy was my locker full of immaculately folded and hung uniform on my glorious wooden hangers, cheers Mum!

The inspections were brutal but there was always a game to be played. Sneaking something into someone's locker last minute that the DS would find and trying not to smirk was common. Or the DS themselves asking you hilarious questions while you stood to attention, adding the additional pressure to not give in and smile; if you smirked, they shouted. I was also now getting used to just being a surname. 'Aircrew Cadet McConaghy', or MAC for short by the regiment DS who were a little less formal. Oh, and when you messed up it was quite simply, 'McCONAGHY' at full volume. We began to learn drill on the parade square, which was right up there with rank slides in terms of difficulty to grasp. Ironically, as I moved through my forces life the ranks became second nature to recognise, I cannot say the same for drill manoeuvres. This is where Grohly came into his own. One of his previous jobs with the RAF regiment was duty on the 'Queens Colour Squadron' or QCS for short and lovingly referred to as 'the gun jugglers'. These are the guys who guard the keys at the Tower of London and who do ceremonial duties. More importantly, whom I had seen years ago on a TV challenge programme called 'YOU BET' where they had performed drill commands to music. As well as this being entertaining to watch, their drill was immaculate. Dave spent our initial weekends teaching myself and a few other 'slow learners' drill in the car park outside the block. We weren't allowed off camp for the first three weeks, which in hindsight was a godsend and we used our time wisely. It also meant that the only shop we could visit was the NAAFI just a few minutes' walk from our accommodation. I popped down there the first Sunday to get biscuits to thank Dave. What was the first thing I spied on entering? A wall of wooden coat hangers for sale!

So, drill was coming along nicely, I was pretty adept at making bed packs, and I was saluting anything that moved. The next big hurdle was the physical training sessions. Now as I have already alluded, I was definitely not in peak fitness on joining up. What did not help the matter either was that our issue PT kit was horrendous. White T-shirt with your name on it and the shortest, white, creased shorts all topped off with a very bland pair of the most useless trainers known to man: 'the silver shadow'. They haunt me to this day. I dreaded every PT session as I was ALWAYS the fat lass at the back on the runs around Cranwell and up 'cardiac hill' which was true to its name. The PTs didn't take any prisoners when it came to my lack of fitness. We had to take pine poles on some of our runs, carrying them on your shoulder with a teammate and they routinely dished me out the biggest one. This, however, again made me tougher, stronger, and more tenacious, always the last to finish, but I always finished!

As the weeks of drill and pine-pole carrying went on, my shoulders became black and blue. I ended up having to tape socks under my sports bra straps and winced each time we were given the command to slope arms as this meant slamming your rifle into your shoulder. I had blisters on all sides of my feet and was constantly tired, but I still carried on; giving up would have been harder. I also distinctly remember my first day shooting a live SA80 on the range. We had spent weeks learning how to dismantle and rebuild the weapon, learning what to do when it jammed or misfired and also the 'marksmanship' principles that were drilled into us to help us to actually hit a target 200m away. I say 'actually' as it was mostly pure fluke that I hit anything from that day onwards as the marksmanship principles immediately escaped me. I do recall it was something about breathing and holding the weapon in natural alignment, but I also realise, looking back now, how little I would need them when it mattered. On passing my weapon-handling test in the classroom I was deemed safe enough to be allowed to shoot the SA80 for real. I was on the second 'detail' to shoot that day and therefore was sitting outside the huge wall of the range waiting for my turn. It's something all soldiers take for granted now but the very first time you hear the 'crack' of a weapon it shocks you. We watch movies all the time with guns being fired and see reports on the news, but it instantly cuts through your thoughts when you hear a bullet being fired for real. Something that sadly became more and more familiar to me as my career went on.

As the weeks went by, we were finally allowed out of camp at weekends. Most people went home to see their family or loved ones, but there was a small bunch of four misfits who always stayed behind. This was mainly as we just couldn't easily travel home. Obviously, I was from N.I; Dave had been stationed at RAF Aldergrove N.I prior to the course so was a rolling stone; and the other guys were from the Shetlands and the Isle of Man. Both helpfully called George and, shall we say, both 'unique'. But the big bonus was that they were both teetotal. Result! Most weekends Grohly and I would spend Saturday afternoons shopping and wandering around in Lincoln. I could finally buy some 'going out' clothes and high heels, approved by Dave, and he would always buy a very dapper new shirt, the ones with the white cuffs and collars were very popular back then. We'd then head home to the block, get our glad rags on and the four of us would head into Lincoln with either of the Georges driving. We had the best nights, 19 years old, getting paid £500 a month with nothing to spend it on except clothes and shoes, chips and booze. Our favourite game was to come out of Ritzies the nightclub and head to the 'Sarnie Shack' for food before home. The staff all had T-shirts that said 'we do NOT serve chips' emblazoned on them. You guessed it, we always asked for chips. As did a few other strangers in the queue ahead or behind us, who we instantly knew were also from Cranwell by this obvious annoying question to the staff.

One of my funniest memories of Grohly and basic training was this, however. We had a joint commune room in our block where we lived and someone had set some blackcurrant jelly in a pint glass, so it looked as though it was three-quarters full of blackcurrant squash. It was the running joke for a few days to pretend to throw it at people as they walked in through the door and watch them flinch. But eventually the novelty wore off and the glass remained stagnant on the windowsill. Towards the end of our basic training course, we decided to have a course night into Lincoln. All of us for a change on a Thursday night. We all convened in the commune room prior to getting our taxis from the main gate. Most of us were sitting in the room ready to go and waiting for Grohly, who was busy making himself immaculate as always – the best dressed straight man I know. Perfectly pressed shirt, well-chosen shoes and belt and hair coiffured to within an inch of its life. As he walked through the door, I thought it would be funny to do the old pint glass trick and picked it up and pretended to throw the contents of the glass towards him. What I hadn't banked on was the same joker who had put the jelly in the pint glass had swapped it for ACTUAL blackcurrant squash. Grohly looked on in horror as I covered his white shirt in dark purple juice! The worst bit, however, was that I was so surprised myself I just started laughing, uncontrollably. I couldn't even speak to explain or apologise, so to all intents and purposes Grohly thought the whole thing was premeditated and just stood there, dripping in disbelief. Good job he loved me, and he has put up with me and my bad decisions ever since …

The overall theme throughout basic training was to create leaders out of us. We weren't just basic recruits to be spat out as junior ranks, we would graduate as sergeants, which is a respectable rank. The reasoning behind this was so that we would have a level of rank above most of the troops we flew when we were briefing them etc. Therefore, our training contained many tasks and exercises, some at Cranwell, some further afield where we were always given a scenario as our nominated 'lead'. When it was your turn, you got a 'task brief' from the DS, then briefed your team on the 'mission', appointed a second in command, and various other roles. The command tasks were all inventive but usually revolved around getting from A to B on a time limit and then building something, ALWAYS out of pine poles which we carried. By week nine we deployed up to an exercise area called Otterburn, north of Newcastle for Exercise Southern Border. This was our first test with a pass or fail leadership element. It was gruelling. I had blisters from the first day and the weather was awful. Plus, we were all living in 12ft by 12ft field tents, so it was impossible to dry your kit. I didn't do so well during this in terms of my leadership tests. 'Room for improvement' is how I would best describe it. Despite having lots of people to teach me the raw elements of military life, leadership is an extremely difficult skill to teach. I truly believe it's either in you or it's not.

After Southern Border it was back to Cranwell, or Cranditz as we lovingly referred to it now, for a few more weeks of consolidation training prior to the final test in week 11. Exercise Border Patrol was the infamous last hurdle of the course. During this you had to get two satisfactory passes at Leadership then complete a run with Bergens (our large military-issue rucksacks) and pine poles on your shoulders and only after that would the staff make their decision in conjunction with your overall performance as to whether you graduated or not. I managed, somehow to pull both my 'leads' out of the bag as satisfactory, mostly as my course mates were amazing and really rallied around to help me. Being the 'one with the great personality' and a proper little teammate, was finally paying off. Last thing was the run. Even as we set off every part of me ached. I still had socks taped under my sports bra straps on both shoulders as they were so battered and bruised. That run was the hardest thing I had done in my life. I was always at the back of the pack the whole way, over relentless hills, knees hurting, lungs screaming and then eyes streaming as I began to cry. I could see the finish point and all the DS standing there, along with all my course mates who had already finished. I just kept repeating to myself, failure is not an option. I had set off from NI to follow my dream, I had no plan B. I can't tell you if it was the lust to succeed or the fear of failure, but something kept me going that day. The DS clapped as I collapsed over the finish line.

Now despite passing all the tests on the final exercise, my fate still lay in the hands of the Officer DS cadre. They would hold a round table and decide each of our fates individually by basically voting in or out. The dreaded 'Black Tuesday' loomed, which is when we would be told who had made it. That morning I felt sick, I just had a gut feeling that they thought I was still too young and naïve and would benefit from going through the course one more time. Truth be told, so did I. After lunch they got us to all stand in a circle facing outwards, with our backs to the door of our classroom. The instructions were, if they called your name, you turned around, saluted, and went back to your bed space, you had been re-coursed and would be starting again the following week. The names began, some not so surprising then one guy's name was called that shocked me, as I was sure he would pass. Instantly I knew my name would be next as if he hadn't made it there was no hope I had. The next words I heard them say were: 'The rest of you remaining will be graduating. Congratulations.' Little Lizzy from Newtownards had done it. Well, I'll be damned. That afternoon we had our end of course interviews with the Course Leader Flight Lieutenant Brown. At the end of mine he stood up and looked me right in the eye, held out his hand for me to shake and said, 'You know what McConaghy, I'm really, really proud of you, I didn't think you would make it,' and smiled. I thought the exact same thing as I shook his hand and said, 'Thank you sir,' saluted and walked out to begin the best life imaginable.

Chapter 3

Getting Closer to 'That'

A week later, the day before my Graduation Parade, my mum, dad and little brother flew over from Northern Ireland to Cranwell. They hate travelling and my dad loathes flying so it was a big deal for them, but obviously they were beside themselves with excitement. That evening I took them out for dinner; I'd grown up a great deal since they'd last set eyes on their little girl.

There was a restaurant I had noticed next to the roundabout on the way into Sleaford, the local town; it always looked busy, so I decided to take them there. After dinner I left them back at the hotel and headed back to camp to prepare my No. 1 uniform and give my shoes a last good polish in the common room with everyone else. Old tights are surprisingly great for this, so we were constantly dishing them out to the lads. Grohly asked if my parents had arrived OK etc. and I announced to the room that yes, they had, and I'd taken them out for a lovely dinner in that nice restaurant down the road called 'The Little Chef'! They all burst out laughing. We didn't have food chains like Little Chef back home, so I had no idea why this was so hilarious and receiving so much banter. I obviously do now ...

The morning of the Graduation came, and I opened the curtains to see, nothing. Yep, it was thick December fog, and you could barely see the parade square. Nevertheless, we formed up as the graduating Flight outside the block as our loved ones took their seats on the grandstand at the parade square. Out we marched to the band of the RAF in our No.1s looking tip-top and I can honestly say the hairs on the back of my neck stood up; I was brimming with pride. I was marching with my course mates – who had helped me through the last twelve weeks successfully – and, thankfully, was not back in the block waiting for round two. Thank God I was in the front rank of the parade as the fog was so thick my parents could only just see that row, everyone behind me, including the band, were now figures in the mist ... and sadly the flypast that had been booked for our big day had to cancel. After the parade it was back to the warrant officers' and sergeants' mess to show our families our new living accommodation. We were served a slap up three-course lunch in the mess, with a string quartet playing in the corner. Oh my days, I felt proud to show my mum and dad my new 'company' and essentially home. I do not eat fish, never have, and guess what we were served? Prawn cocktail, followed by sea bass. My mum and dad could not believe how posh it all was, while I delicately pushed the fish around for an hour. Thankfully, dessert was Eton mess which still remains my favourite to this day, but once again a new thing for me as up until then I had never even heard of it. Despite the fog, the flypast no show and the fish-induced famine, nothing could spoil that day for me. It was amazing.

After the Christmas break, it was back to Cranwell but this time to live with all our mates in the sergeants' mess. It was an old building full of history with three 'wings' of rooms, joint showers, a dining room, TV room, sitting room and a bar! Yep, we had a bar that served a pint for less than a pound and a Southern Comfort and diet Coke, my drink of choice, for 45p and it was under our very own roof. It also had its own juke box and snooker table. This could get messy, excuse the pun, and it did. Imagine living with all your mates, and the courses ahead of you, roughly all same age, all fairly well paid, and with cheap drinks. It was like being at university but without the beans on toast and the huge debt! We spent many a night gathered in the bar drinking until the small hours, playing killer pool and silly bar games. My favourite was that in the bar at Cranwell you could just about get the entire way around the room without touching the floor. We had so many laughs at 4 a.m. watching people take leaps of faith from the bar to the nearest set of wall seats, or stacking it off the railings beside the juke box. The only small downside, if you can call it that, is that some of the older members of the mess didn't particularly like our lot. As I mentioned before, we graduated into the rank of sergeant, this was so we could hold authority when looking after passengers and soldiers on our aircraft. However, this meant that there was a flurry of new 'plastic sergeants', as we were referred to, swarming into the mess every three months, such as me at only 19 years old.

We began our basic loadmaster training down at main building of Cranwell College in the January. This was a mix of ground school, covering rules of the air, and more specific things on how to calculate the weight and balance of an aircraft and some practical 'attempts' at loading one. Hence the job title, Loadmaster, and we had a mock-up of an aircraft in the basement of the college to practise with. At this stage it was still very generic as we were yet to be streamed on to an aircraft type and there were options for us to be sent either to a fixed wing platform such as a Hercules or TriStar, or sent on to helicopters – mainly the Puma or Chinook. This is when I met another person who had a huge influence on my life. My instructor for ground school was 'Big Gibbo'. He was a helicopter man through and through, having flown on Wessex and Chinooks. He had epic stories from his time flying over in Northern Ireland and funnily enough my earliest memories of any helicopter were as a child watching the Wessex display at Newtownards air show. He had also been on the only Chinook that survived when the *Atlantic Conveyor* was torpedoed during the Falklands war. He was a larger-than-life character, always full of banter and I hung on every word and piece of advice he offered. This just cemented how much I wanted to be posted to Chinooks, but it was still not a certainty by any means. He saved my bacon spectacularly one evening when we were away visiting RAF Benson to look at the Puma aircraft and have a little trial flight. That night, we all went out into Wallingford, the nearest town, for a curry as was the RAF tradition seemingly. This was my first ever curry and as I sat there staring at the menu, I had no idea where to start. I piped up to ask for advice and my crewmate Jonah said, 'Well Liz, have you heard the song *Vindaloo*?' I replied that of course I had, and he went on to inform me that this was the mildest curry that most of the UK ate hence why they had written a song about it. As the waiter came round to take my order, I happily asked for a vindaloo not noticing the sniggers from around the table at my imminent downfall. Thankfully, Gibbo just couldn't bring himself to let it happen and intervened. 'She'll have a Chicken Tikka Masala, trust me Liz, just trust me.' And I did, thank God.

At the end of the course, we had to fill in our 'dream sheet' which was basically a wish list of where you wanted posting. I couldn't understand why anyone on my course would have put fixed wing over rotary as to me the helicopter world was the only option for a life of excitement and purpose. As far as I could tell the fixed wing boys and girls just flew around the globe checking into hotels? The hilarity was that I thought that sounded boring! A few, however, thankfully didn't, so they put fixed wing and filled up those slots, and I, clearly having been cheeky and written rotary as option A and B, got my 'dream' and was posted to RAF Shawbury to start on 53 Course Basic Helicopter Training that summer.

Before beginning this next stage of my training there were two things we needed to complete. The first was a course called Mortrek. This was a week of Ray Mears-type survival training. We learnt how to build shelters, collect water, start fires, and catch food. It was during a lovely summery week near Skipton, and we learnt lots of new life skills. Gibbo was one of the instructors who showed us how to skin a rabbit. I still remember him letting me volunteer to do it while the rest of the course watched on. He coached me through it explaining 'it's like peeling off his little pyjamas' and he was right, really easy. We also had a chicken that we had to look after all week then kill it and cook it on our fires during the last day. We were starving by this point having camped in a forest for four days, living on anything we caught, which for me wasn't a lot. So, killing the chicken was pretty easy by this point. My teammate and I put it on the fire and our mouths were watering. He left me to supervise it while he went to collect water. By the time he returned I had burnt it to a crisp, and it tasted like charcoal. He never forgave me, in fact neither did I. My ability to burn water is somewhat renowned amongst my friends even now. I lost nearly a stone in that week and it was my first ever summer ball that Friday night back in the sergeants' mess at Cranwell. I had been looking forward to it all week and thought about how skinny I would look in my new ball gown. You should know by now that things in my life never go as planned though. The last night on Mortrek I had been bitten all over my face by midges while we lay up waiting to be 'simulated rescued'. I woke up on the Friday morning looking like an extra from *Star Trek*. Turns out I'm allergic to midge bites. Ace. I spent the entire morning bathed in camomile lotion, then Kate and Emma decided we needed professional help but not in the form of a doctor. They took me to Debenhams in Lincoln for the make-up counter lady to try her best. She looked at me and I could almost hear her think 'I'm not a magician.' Anyhow, Cinderella did make it to the ball that night in her nice blue ball gown that was slightly loose, but her face now resembled Krusty the Clown with layers of orange foundation trowelled on and bright blue eyeshadow. Barbara Cartland, eat your heart out.

We also had to do the dreaded 'Dunker' or Under Water Helicopter Escape Training, and indeed every three years thereafter. The clue is in the title: basically you get strapped into a helicopter structure then they drop it into the water and you have to escape. There are so many horror stories about people nearly drowning so everyone is always somewhat nervous – even water babies like me. On your first time ever attending, you start with the 'suicide chair'. Great name to install confidence. With this you get strapped into a small cage with a bottle of compressed air and must learn to purge it and then breathe, using it while under the water for a minute. It most definitely induces panic in people and was my least favourite bit. Once you have successfully 'survived' the chair you move on to the helicopter module. The first 'run', as they call it, is with the lights on and you are upright. You all climb in and take your seats and pop your lap strap on. There is a bit of a wait then the module drops so that you are now chest height in the water. This is done to allow you to catch your breath before it fully descends under the water. It's a double-edged sword though, as although it does give you a second or two to catch your composure it feels like an age. You never want to take your last breath too early and overcook it or wait too long and miss the chance. After the first upright run, the next time they roll the frame slightly to simulate a crash, third time it rolls completely upside down, then lastly upside down with the lights turned off. Finally, you finish with some training using the emergency oxygen bottles. Oh joy. The hilarious bit is, while you're waiting in the area upstairs you can watch what's happening to those ahead of you, adding to the anxiety. It's designed to train us for ditching in a helicopter over the sea and we need to complete it if we want to be aircrew. What I haven't said though is that several of you all strap in and when you go under the person seated next to the window must push it out, then you all take turns to swim through the hole. So, you could be sitting there holding your breath for quite some time if you are number 4 along the seat. On one of my last runs, the chap sitting next to me was nominated window man. We went under and I blurrily watched him faff about under the water for what seemed like an age, trying to release the window. I'd had enough, so pushed him aside, popped the window and through I went followed by the rest, then finally him. What a muppet, but lesson learnt: take responsibility for your own survival folks, especially if you're sitting next to the class clown.

With limited spaces on each course, I had to hold for a month or so before getting to Shawbury, where I finally caught up with Grohly who had been loaded on the course ahead of me. This was great as once again he was able to offer help and advice despite this being a new environment for both of us. I was the youngest on my course by ten years. One of my new crewmates on No. 54 course was Dusty Hare, another ex-RAF regiment guy. He lovingly referred to me as 'Sprog', which meant youngster in military speak, or if he was hungover, I was upgraded to 'the screaming skull' due to my never-ending dulcet tones, but I was so lucky again to have found myself among a great bunch of lads. This is where I started to realise just how few women there were in the helicopter crewman world. There were no others on any of the courses ahead or coming behind me and there were no female crewman instructors, but thankfully, when we met our trainee pilots with whom we would be crewed, I met Hannah. She was, and still is, an outstanding example to any woman in the forces with her level headedness and just 'get on with it' attitude. We went through our Shawbury flying course together and the next phase of our Operational Conversion Unit and were posted to our first Operational Squadron together. She runs the Chinook School now and I wish I was still in to be her crewman leader; what an achievement that would have been.

Flying on 60 Squadron at RAF Shawbury was the next step up in terms of challenge as this was when we had to 'up our game' and get things right in the air. I remember the first time I plugged my flying helmet into the intercom of our twin-engine Griffin helicopter to allow us to talk as a crew and listen to the air traffic radios. It was as if when the rotors started turning, they sucked my brain out of my head and I was at maximum capacity. It's a very unique skill to be able to work in this kind of environment and is referred to as CRM or crew resource management. You must not only balance your own intercom so you're not the loudest one speaking, but measure when you speak, be clear on what you say without waffling and not talk over the radios. I was a loud, chatty, bubbly Norn-Irish lass, so you can imagine this took a few sorties to get to grips with, and most of my early sorties were just filled with the instructor shouting 'Radios' at me, which was a sign to shut up as we had ATC info coming through in our earpieces. We were slowly taught in modules how to voice marshall or direct the aircraft around the skies and essentially become the pilot's eyes for certain skills. We landed on slopes, in confined areas that got tighter and more challenging every week and learnt how to successfully, as a crew, pick up an underslung load (USL) that was attached to a hook on the belly of the airframe. We had a right laugh though, and our course all got on really well; it was like being at summer school. We had lots of squadron beer calls, nights out in Shrewsbury and fancy-dress parties in the mess.

There was a set of double doors halfway along the corridor on 60 Squadron where we would wait for our aircraft to return. Anxiously, we would then walk out and crew swap with whichever course mates had been flying before us on the little Bell 214 Griffin helicopters that we used for our training. This area was also where we left our kit bags for the odd overnight land-away we did as part of the course. There we developed the rule 'never leave your kit unattended' which I have lived by ever since. The reason for this was that you never knew what would be added, such as heavy bricks etc. or indeed removed from your kit bag when it was left alone. By far the most annoying thing that could be done was for someone to remove one shoe from your overnight 'dancing rig'. Yes, just one shoe, not the pair. This was because it was more annoying to unpack getting ready to go out and realise that you hadn't forgotten to pack your shoes, as could be the case if both were missing, but in fact that you had packed them, and some joker had nicked one! It was common to see aircrew out in bars around the country in their 'out out' clothes avec black flying boots. Priceless.

I surprised myself by how well I did on the course and managed to sail through with relative ease, despite having one of the hardest old-school crewmen 'Amos Bell' as an instructor. I look back now though and realise that Amos saw in me what Big Gibbo and Flight

Lieutenant Brown had, and that was 'potential'. I may not have been the cleverest, but I always gave it my best, always listened to debriefs and was most definitely a team player.

Much like before, at the end of the course we had to fill in our 'dream sheets', so they could try and match our next posting to which aircraft we wanted. There is always one big caveat with this and that is they must fill the gaps on the front line, so 'Service Need' is always the main driver. Now, in order for us to find out what our destiny would be, we had what was called 'a role disposal'. This involves a little challenge or assault course of some description out at the front of 60 Squadron's building with a lot of beer involved and ending with you necking a pint on which your new aircraft type is written at the bottom of the glass. It usually also results in a lot of this beer being thrown over your head, as the military have a ritual that the second you start to neck a pint on one of these socials, they begin to count down from ten. What you have not finished by the time they all shout 'one', then goes 'on your head' and you must 'self-pour' what remains in the glass over yourself from above. So off I go for my little assault attempt, beginning with a few rotations of a pole so I'm adequately dizzy, under a cargo net, over some obstacles, then back to my pint to neck it, pour it on my head and excitedly look into the empty glass. The word written at the bottom was 'Merlin'. Yep, I had been posted to Merlins, the new RAF helicopter that they were desperately trying to get crews on to. I was gutted, properly gutted but clearly couldn't cry as the whole squadron were now cheering and clapping. Off goes Dusty for his turn and he gets the same. Also gutted. Once the shenanigans had started to die down and the BBQ was lit, the crewman leader pulled us both over to the sidelines for a chat. I assumed he was going to apologise as he knew we had both been posted to an aircraft that we didn't want, but for me it was more than that, my dream had been demolished. He began by saying that the Merlins were really struggling at the minute to get people through and as such there was a backlog. I expected his next sentence would be 'So you're going to be holding for a while before you go.' But he announced, 'So actually because they are so far behind, despite being posted to Merlins on paper you will both be going to Chinooks as they have just told us they can take you and will make space for you on their next course.' I had been saved by a twist of fate, but now believed even more it was always my destiny to head to the mighty Wokka. To say more drinks were consumed that evening would be an understatement ...

Chapter 4

Belonging

In July 2003, I arrived at RAF Odiham to begin No. 24 Chinook Operational Conversion Flight, OCF for short. We spent the first few weeks at RAF Benson covering ground school which came in the format of sitting in a building from 0800 to 1700 daily learning Chinook tech by computer. The Chinook is a complex aircraft so there was a lot to learn. I joke now that I can change the battery in a Chinook but have no idea how to do it in my car and that's the truth. It's our job as crewmen to know the ins and outs of every system on board, not only so we can try and fix it when it goes wrong in the air but also as we are the ones who service it when we land away from base. You need to get this right as lives can depend on it. It was intense and happened to be one of the hottest summers on record so each night when we went back to the hotel, we would all take a much-needed dip in the Thames which ran past our hotel in Oxford. There was a bridge right outside the hotel and we decided it would be fun to jump off the bridge into the river. We were all standing there ready to go until someone piped up, 'I wonder how deep it is?' Doubt crept in, what if we jumped the 20ft or so and it was only 4ft deep! Seconds later, Tarq just went for it, in the classic crewman way shouting 'fuck it'! As soon as he surfaced in one piece the rest of us leapt off! A few months later, there was a wedding at the same hotel. One of the guests jumped off the same bridge, drunk, during the evening do. He hit a shopping trolley and killed himself. Another life lesson: if you think something might be a bad idea it probably is; don't be easily led. That summer, however, was when my course mates became like best friends. We had all been through various stages of training at different times, but now we were finally aligned again with one thing in common: Chinooks.

Then it was time to start the good stuff: flying on the amazing Wokka. The Operational Conversion Unit (OCU) was designed to convert you on to type from your basic helicopter training. Now this would be straightforward had I been posted to Merlin or Puma helicopters, as both of these only have one hook to attach a USL to, and they both have a tail rotor like the Griffin we were used to. However, the Chinook is a mightier beast. It has three USL hooks (and can lift heavier, therefore more complicated, things beneath), and two rotor heads so its flying characteristics are totally different and unique. Now my 'office' space inside was big enough to winch or drive anything in, from a Land Rover or 105 field gun, through to boats, cars, trailers, motorbikes, donkeys … basically if you could fit it in over the ramp you could carry it, and if not, you could put it in a net and pick it up on your hooks. Lots to learn but I was 'becoming'. I was finally becoming 'that'. The thing I had always wanted to be and if I'm totally honest until the Chinook OCU I didn't really grasp just how awesome a job it would be. Then of course comes the moment that still makes me the envy of nearly every man I know: the aircraft gunnery sorties. The Chinook is fitted with two different air-to-ground weapons: the M60 which was used on Huey helicopters back in Vietnam and which we had fitted to the ramp, and the M134 or 'minigun' as it is known. This always struck me as a hilarious name, as with a fire rate of 3,000 rounds of 7.62 calibre per minute, taking seconds to destroy any target, there is F– all 'mini' about it! We call it the 'crowd pleaser' and I must admit, every time I heard it open fire it brought a smile to my face … or at least it did until I had to use it in anger.

There was an instructor on the OCU called Roly. He had just returned from his instructor course and we were his first students. I don't know how, but I always seemed to be allocated the harshest instructors and Roly was exactly that. He didn't pull any punches, and this was the first time I ever felt as though someone was being harder on me for being a girl. And looking back he was, but for good reason. He was building me up to cut the mustard in the man's world of the Chinook fleet. On one of our night sorties, we were practising picking up a 105 field gun. I had my night vision goggles (NVG) fitted and was operating as the No.2 crewman who is positioned at the front door of the cabin. My course mate Tom was positioned in the centre hatch which is where the No.1 crewman carries out his duties, as well as the ramp area. Roly was our instructor and because what we were doing was an advanced skill, he was positioned with Tom by the centre hatch to supervise. As we began to take up the tension on the centre strop attached to the hook, it was my job to bring the step in at the front. Then go and check on the left to make sure we were 'clear above and behind' to lift into the air, before heading back to the door for lookout. As I arrived and leant on to the door it gave way. Out I went, head first, 40ft high at night. Thankfully, my harness stopped me just as I hit the 45-degree point. So, I was now hanging out of the aircraft with my feet still inside, knees on the step, staring at the 40ft drop beneath me. I managed to reach up to my comms lead and key 'hot mic' so I could speak.

'Erm Roly.'

'Yes Liz.'

'Can you come and get me?'

'What you mean Liz?'

'Well, I'm hanging outside the front door.'

He instantly unplugged his intercom and headed towards me, but I could hear the air turn bluer as he got nearer, even over the noise of the aircraft rotors. For a split second I thought it may be less painful to release my harness and plummet to my impending doom rather than face the wrath of Roly. He pulled me in, checked I was OK and asked if I wanted to carry on the sortie. I did. This was not the first nor the last time Roly had to rescue me, but although I knew he would, I always remained scared when the time came.

OCU complete, another dream sheet was presented with the choice of three squadrons: 18, 27 or 7 Squadron. Now 7 Squadron was the Special Forces Squadron at Odiham which flew the SAS (Special Air Service) and SBS (Special Boat Service) guys, and generally as a rule you wouldn't dream of even asking to go straight from the OCU; you had to learn your trade first. It was also known, but not said out loud, that much like a Yorkie bar, it was not for girls. This sounds ridiculous in today's world of equal rights, but in the environments they worked and lived in, I still to this day think that the Special Forces world should remain men only. The OCU operated out of 18 Squadron's building at the time, so all our instructors worked in that building and used the crew room daily. I wanted a fresh start, to arrive on a squadron that knew me as the new crew gal without the preconceived judgement from crew-room instructor chat, so I put 27 Squadron down as my first choice. Once again, my wish was granted so off I went. It also helped that 27 Squadron was closer to the sergeants' mess and that their morning brief was at 0830 rather than 18 Squadron's which was 0815. Win, win, extra fifteen minutes in bed every day!

So, first day on 27 Squadron, myself, and Tarqs the other crewman who was on my course met at breakfast and walked over together. Rule number one, day one: stick together. We met the other pilots who were also coming to 27 at the door and headed in together – safety in numbers. Hannah had also been posted here so we had now increased the female count of aircrew on the squadron to two. That's right, we were now the only two females on the squadron. It was definitely better having both of us arrive at the same time. That said, the lads never treated us any differently. I had learnt pretty well by now you get far more respect for not trying to highlight yourself as being 'special' in any way: as a chick doing such a manly job, and in shouting about it, you single your own self out in a sexist way. If you think you are owed some sort of prize for being capable of doing things as a woman, you're almost saying you are incapable in the first place. Keep your head down, get stuck in the same as the rest and be the best 'person' at your job. But the most important thing to accept is that sometimes you may have to ask for help, but that does not make you weak. If I genuinely wasn't strong enough to do something the way the lads did, such as carry a 5m USL strop over my shoulder I would adapt to dragging it as required. I got the task done in my own way. If I couldn't lift something heavy inside the cabin, I would ask my crewmate to help. But it goes both ways, if they couldn't reach up inside an engine to check out a filter as their hands were too large, I would do it. If they couldn't slide past a Land Rover we had strapped down inside, off I shimmied. It's about playing to your strengths to get the job done and most importantly teamwork.

When we had been going through all our various courses to this point, we as students would stick together and it was us versus the staff. But now on the squadron there was most definitely an established crewman vs pilot 'friendly' mentality. You want a job done, go ask a crewman. You need help, go ask a crewman. The junior pilots were warned about the so-called crewman mafia and how you didn't want to get on the wrong side of them. This 'thick as thieves' mafia became my family throughout all my years thereafter, just like a real mafia would. They looked after me like a little sister. The crewmen brethren are the tightest brotherhood you will ever come across. We always stick together, and I have seen first-hand how miserable they can make a pilot's life if they take a dislike to them. Generally, though, if the crewmen gave you a nickname as a young pilot you were golden; even if it was obscenely offensive, which most of the time it was, you would take it and embrace it with open arms. If you tried to shake a nickname, it was guaranteed to stay with you for life.

This whole 'team' ethos was the biggest difference I found with finally being on a squadron. I belonged. I had an identity and a bunch of people who looked out for me as one of 'theirs'. I was on A Flight, but Tarqs went to B Flight and there was a healthy internal squadron rivalry between the two flights. Mostly in the form of beer calls and drinking games or the odd footy match etc., but ultimately it was just a numbers game, and we all did the same job. We did, however, deploy as Flights, so we got to know our own much better. There was also rivalry between the other two squadrons, which again mostly manifested itself in drinking races at dinner nights, and some squadron emblems being painted around camp. One of my favourites was when 18 Squadron painted their very large black and red Pegasus emblem on our squadron boss's garage in the middle of the night, which he walked out to discover the next morning. Our squadron emblem was an elephant with green, red, and yellow, so we painted between the yellow lines around the station with a red stripe down the middle then filled in the car park spaces out the front of the officers' mess with green, yellow and red. A genius one was 27 Squadron painting a huge elephant on the roof of 18 Squadron's building so that when they came into land this was all they could see. Great fun.

This rivalry got even better amongst the other helicopter fleets. We would routinely land away to stay overnight at their bases at RAF Benson and Aldergrove and leave our squadron elephant stamp behind somewhere, as did 18 Squadron with their Pegasus, as we were all now on 'Team Chinook'. The Puma and Merlin guys of course did the same. I remember taxiing out one Monday morning to Eastern 2 helipad to take off, only for us to discover a huge tiger had been spray-painted by a 230 Squadron, Puma crew who had landed at Odiham over the weekend. Fair play boys. Things would get 'borrowed' from crew rooms, mugs would be kidnapped etc., but it was all good healthy Support Helicopter (SH) banter. By far the most hilarious and outstanding one of all was this though. An 18 Squadron crew had been on task over in Northern Ireland and been working out of RAF Aldergrove. They finished the task and departed on the Sunday evening to return to Odiham. Now, as mentioned above, 230 Squadron at Aldergrove are the Tiger Squadron and have a huge historical back catalogue that goes with that. This also includes the famous life-size brass tiger statue that is their pride and joy and sits as thus, just inside their crew-room door. Monday morning arrives and the Officer Commanding (OC) 18 Squadron receives a rather agitated, 'OK that's an understatement', livid phone call from OC 230 Squadron. 'BRING ME BACK MY TIGER' is the easiest way to sum up what was undoubtedly a slightly more colourful conversation, shall we say. OC 18 Squadron then immediately calls said crew up via the squadron tannoy system, to his office. 'Bring your berets', which means you know you are in for more than just a quick chat. He then begins to deliver the appropriately required bollocking to the four crew, while trying not to laugh. Rumour has it he shook their hands at the end of said 'bollocking'. Priceless, for everything else there's Master Card! And yes, 230 Squadron did get their tiger back eventually. I cannot confirm what may have happened to it in the few days it was on its mini break to Odiham, but I can hazard a guess.

All the while that I was on 27 Squadron, I lived in the sergeants' mess at Odiham. A lot of my mates lived in there as well, so we had a great social life. It did, however, give rise to some hilarious incidents regarding my pants. By this stage I had upgraded from my pre-RAF white Bridget Jones specials and now pretty much lived in black underwear only, to save any further pant-flashing moments. One Friday afternoon, there was a knock on my room door, and I opened it to find one of my older crewmates standing there holding my pants in his hand asking 'are these yours?' It was a fairly safe assumption as I was the only female living in the mess at the time and lived on the same corridor! I was mortified and grabbed them from him, instantly turning bright red! 'Yes, they are, where did you find them?' Turns out he had his 'Mrs' coming to stay for the weekend. He had done the decent thing and put his bedding in the wash that morning and then into the tumble dryer. At lunchtime he decided rather than just leaving it on the bed he would go all out and actually make the bed up for her! Push the boat out eh! Upon doing this he had discovered my pants, lurking inside his duvet cover! How did they get there one may ask? Well, that's what you get when you all share the same laundry room one after another! Thank God, he found them as there is no way you could easily explain that one away!

The next incident happened a few months later. Flying suits are designed with a zip located on the inside of the lower leg. I've actually no idea what these zips are for, but I can only assume so you can get your flying suit on and off over your boots. I've never tried, nor needed to. But the zip also has a little Velcro strap that sits across it. One morning, with my freshly washed flying suit on, pens relocated in the pockets and Velcro badges placed back on, off I went to work. I spent the morning running around doing bits and bobs and then back to the mess for lunch. After lunch we always headed to catch up in the crew room for a brew. I jumped up on the large seat we had, which was an old engine on its end with a padded cushion on top. I was happily sitting there chatting away when someone asked … 'are those your pants?' I looked down to discover I had indeed been walking around the squadron and indeed camp all day dragging my pants along by my ankle. Hand in the cool badge once and for all McC.

There was a further 'pant on show' incident many years later on Op Herrick. When we are deployed on Ops we wear combats to fly in rather than flying suits. This is mainly so if we go down behind enemy lines we can blend in as a ground troop rather than be identifiable as aircrew and possibly interrogated as such. The odd person seemed to want to wear a flying suit, which I never really understood. No matter how 'cool' you want to look walking around camp, the novelty would wear off pretty damn quickly if you had to go on the run in the Helmand Valley. The other thing is the issued desert flying suits were a horrible shade of pink in colour and didn't fare well when mixed with sweat and dust so the two-piece combats were always my flying kit of choice, plus it was much easier to go for a tinkle quickly as flying suits are not designed for women in this respect. One particular morning, I got airborne and during the first hour of flying managed to tear a huge rip in the backside of my combats on a ballistic protection panel fitted to the floor. I was the No.1 crewman therefore seated on the ramp and manning the M60 throughout the day, hence why the accident happened in the first place. We had a full day's tasking ahead so no option to get a new set of combat trousers on. Despite many attempts to 'bodge tape' the rip back up with 'black nasty', as we called it, the large angular rip kept reappearing, displaying my little black thong to anyone and everyone we had on board and was pointed out by most of the lads sitting near the ramp on every pick-up while they giggled. Well let it never be said that Liz McConaghy didn't look after her troops and ensure morale was high at all times.

Chapter 5

Babe in Iraq

When you get posted to a squadron from the OCF you arrive as Limited Combat Ready (LCR). This basically means you still have a lot to learn, especially when it comes to operating the Chinook in a combat zone. There is a training package designed to show you the self-defence systems in depth, and how to operate more quickly and slickly when loading the aircraft and picking up USLs. It's like having training pants on before you get your big girls' pants issued. I was soon to hone these skills with my first deployment to the Falklands, which is a weird place but stunningly beautiful. The day I flew out with my crew, my other instructor crewmate discovered he had forgotten his passport when he arrived at RAF Brize Norton to check in! This resulted in me heading down south without a wingman, but thankfully the outgoing crewmen already there met me at the airhead and took me under their wing. Our aircraft was also greeted by a man dressed in a tiger suit at the side of the runway. This apparently was always done by one of the 78 squadron engineers or crewmen to welcome the new arrivals to the island – clearly too much spare time on their hands. There was a saying at the time that you went to the Falklands and got 'Fit or Fat' as there was nothing to do but go to the gym, or the bar, of which there were many. No, in fact that's another understatement, there were loads! Every section on station had their own, so each night it was off to a different one. Eventually, my other crewmate arrived, and we added some flying into the mix. I don't think I've flown so consistently hungover since then, but it was work hard, play hard. The best bit was that I really got to learn my trade. There are very few roads in the Falklands, so everything is moved around by the Chinook. That is rations, beer, post, gym equipment, ISO containers – you name it. Getting the tasking sheet at the start of the day and trying to decipher what exactly we were taking to where was always fun, and I was given the task of coming up with the plan. I loved it. There was an element of boredom and cabin fever for those stationed at the main base, Mount Pleasant, so everyone always wanted to come flying with us. The Chinook crew were like rock stars and were always invited to parties! What a way to begin a career. I came back six weeks later, fat … well not that fat but I had rediscovered some of the curves I had lost during basic training. Ironically, the Falklands was my first detachment and when I went again for winter 2016 it was my last flying detachment, but more of that later.

All too soon it was back to 27 Squadron to spend a few months in the UK flying with Roly again who was now back as the squadron instructor. He would specifically get me added as crew for the more challenging sorties so I could get as much experience as possible. On one morning a task came into 27 Squadron Ops for a crew to go and under sling a Royal Navy Sea King that had suffered a tip strike on its blades up in the Lake District and fly it back to Prestwick. Roly convinced the hierarchy to let me go on the task with him, despite it being a huge challenge and one that we couldn't afford to get wrong as the aircraft is obviously an expensive bit of kit and must be picked up carefully. They authorised me to go, with Roly's supervision. When we arrived at the Lakes, Roly allowed me to carry out the pick-up. He clearly watched me like a hawk, ready to step in at a moment's notice, but he had the faith in my ability to give it a shot. That's a lesson I always took into my time as an instructor. The best thing you can ever do for your student is believe in them. Of course, they may make a mistake, but if you always do the challenging things for them, how will they ever learn. If you are not given the chance to make these mistakes you will never grow as an operator. The pick-up went really well but the Sea King did not appreciate being attached to a 40-ft strop beneath our Chinook and kept misbehaving in the airflow so the fastest we could fly it was 45 knots. This in turn led to all sorts of fuel calculations on the way to Prestwick as we were now flying much more slowly, therefore airborne for longer than we had anticipated. And because you need a set of ground handlers in place when you attach a load like this, it's not quite as simple as swinging into the nearest airfield to land and get fuel as you now have a bloody great big Sea King attached beneath you, which once it is released needs a whole lot of effort to reattach! I learnt so much that day from that task and all the crew really believed in me and let me make the calculations etc. When we finally arrived at Prestwick, Streety the pilot made the radio call 'One Chinook in close formation with a Sea King.' The air traffic controller replied with 'How close is the Sea King?' To which Streety replied 'about 40 feet!' We all giggled as we knew there was a massive think-bubble now going on in the ATC tower while they looked up out of the window to see us arriving. When we set the Sea King down it began to move. The brakes that should have been tied on back in the field in the Lakes had shaken loose and therefore as we set the aircraft down it began to roll under its own momentum. We couldn't pick it up again, despite it still being attached, as it would have developed a massive swing beneath us. We also couldn't hold it with our aircraft's power as this thing weighed about 8 tonnes. So, we had to carefully release the stoppage we were attached to it by, ensuring that we didn't drop it on to the tail of the helicopter which would have damaged it. The next minute should have had some Benny Hill music overlaid to it as we watched a few engineers chase down this rolling helicopter, in an attempt to stop it making a break for the main runway. One chap threw his hard hat under the front wheel which the heavy aircraft just rolled straight over. Another chap made it as far as grabbing the handle for the cockpit door to swing it open, while a third chap ran over the man now being dragged by the handle he refused to let go of and heroically jumped into the cockpit to pull the brakes on. We couldn't stop laughing at the scene unfolding beneath us, but we had done our job well, and had even been outrun by a flock of geese that day as well, which was another first!

Now I must mention that Roly was infamous amongst the Chinook world. A thick Welsh accent and a very dry and somewhat twisted sense of humour. If there was a leader of the 27 Squadron mafia it was Roly. He continued to be tough on me, always. He asked me tech questions when we were flying and if I got the answers wrong, he made me do press ups on the ramp while the pilot pulled in some collective, resulting in G-forces pressing against me, making the press ups nigh-on impossible. I could bank on him shouting at me every day on 27 Squadron and I used to dash past his office every morning in the hope he wouldn't see me. Inevitably, before I made it to the safety of the blue double doors into the crew room, I would hear his distinctive Welsh accent scream 'McConaghy' at the top of his voice. I would then trot back to hear what fun and games he had in store for me and spend the rest of the day explaining to my mates that I hadn't actually done anything wrong, this was just how he summonsed me. Now this all sounds pretty harsh, and truth be told it was at the time and I hated him.

But he always looked after me when I needed it. Especially during one of our pre-deployment exercises to Morocco. We were staying in a hotel called the Sango, which was fairly rare for helicopter crews as usually we were accommodated in tents. The Sango was pretty nice, it had a lovely pool and slide and the usual cheesy music playing around the pool area from 10 a.m. The only downside was that every morning we had to kick the local cats out of the big bowls of cereal. Now that really should have been enough for most of us to avoid the cornflakes or indeed anything that hadn't been boiled or burnt for cleansing, but we didn't. This resulted in around 90 per cent of the deployment coming down with D and V. On one particular night we were all returning to the hotel from a group night out in Marrakech for dinner at a place called Le Comptoir. As we walked through the lobby, Roly shouted 'all crewmen in the bar, ten minutes, no excuses.' I headed back up to my room and felt very queasy all of a sudden. I lay down on the bed and closed my eyes then a few minutes later the phone by the bed rang. I didn't answer. Then it rang again and again. Eventually, I answered and Roly said 'get your ass down the bar McConaghy' and hung up. I lay back down. A few minutes later the door to my hotel started banging loudly. I could hear Roly hollering so I got up and shuffled to the door. As soon as I opened it, I said 'Roly I don't feel very—' and before I could get the last word out, vomited all over him. If I hadn't been in such a bad way, I could have found this funny, but I was in turmoil. He instantly grabbed me and managed to get me into the small bathroom by the door. I pretty much stayed there and on my bed for the next four days. But in the background Roly had set up a little rota for the crewmen to come check on me every few hours. He was almost like an annoying big brother who just wanted the best for me. I didn't realise this at the time though and for many years after I would do anything to avoid him around station and we had a very love-hate relationship. But I always knew he was the making of me as a crewman. He hardened me and helped me become the best crewman I could be. He would never accept anything less than what he knew I was capable of. Roly believed in me. The last time I saw him was at a mate's wedding in 2015 when I went to the bar and despite best efforts could not avoid bumping into him. We chatted for a bit, and he said he was so proud of the crewman I had become and was pleased to see me settled in life. I never saw him again. Roly was killed in a Puma crash in Kabul that October. I remember the morning after the crash as though it was yesterday. My connected network of friends had been made aware that a Puma had crashed in theatre, and I spent the evening at home waiting to hear if it was anyone I knew well who had been killed. I never even considered Roly as he had always been such a huge part of my Chinook life that I had completely forgotten he had transferred recently on to the Puma fleet. I arrived at the squadron the next morning and as I walked down towards the entrance a very good friend of both Roly and me, Morris, was standing at the door, waiting. He just looked at me and said, 'It was Roly' and I immediately broke down in tears. Morris just wrapped his arms around me into the biggest protective hug he could manage as we both stood there sobbing in silence. It affected me way more than I expected. Roly was my nemesis, but I would not have been the crewman I became without him.

My next deployment away from base was back to home soil in Northern Ireland. By now the troubles were starting to subside since the peace agreement of 1996 had been signed. The army were slowly starting to withdraw from their bases dotted around the province and our task was to under sling a lot of the kit from the mountain sites down at Bessbrook Mill which was a well-established helicopter base with a large ground-force footprint near the Irish border. As a squadron we would head out on a Monday and task through to Friday, then fly back across to Odiham and repeat the following week. I asked gingerly if it would be possible to take my Mini with me one week and stay for the weekend in between to drive home and see my parents. This was one of the huge bonuses of flying on Chinooks, you could, within reason, use the aircraft to the best of its ability for the odd self-gain. I will never forget landing at Aldergrove and reversing my little brown Mini out of the rear of the aircraft on dispersal. The Puma boys from 230 Squadron just stared in awe and as I walked in, said, 'Did a Mini just come out of the back of your Chinook?' Yes, indeed it did my friends, 'Italian job does Aldergrove' go! I also particularly enjoyed my time flying in Northern Ireland as it provided me with the proudest moment of my career very early on and one that was never surpassed. I asked in the tasking office if we could take the aircraft into visit Regent House, my senior school, which my little brother was still attending.

I explained they had a huge cadet force, and it would be brilliant in terms of recruitment etc. After much teeth sucking, the powers that be went from 'No not a chance' to 'Yes that's a great idea for us to relationship-build with the NI public.' That Thursday, off we went to land on the rugby pitches at Regent House School in Newtownards. We shut down and showed more than 1,500 kids around the aircraft, including young ones from the primary school up the road who had walked down to see what was happening! I got to show my little brother and his mates around, my mum and dad, my old school friends and most importantly my granny and granda who would never be able to travel to England to see what I actually did for a living. But the highlight for sure was seeing all the teachers, whom three years previously had told me that I would be wasting my life if I didn't attend university, now asking if they could have a look around my awesome flying office. The party line for the RAF recruitment is #No Ordinary Job, and that day they realised that a career in the forces could be the most diverse and worthwhile career a young adult could embark upon.

While steadily progressing with my Combat Ready work-up training in the UK, the other crews on the squadron were all taking turns to head out to Iraq to carry out their two-month deployment. Every few weeks, new tanned faces would arrive back in the crew room, so despite not feeling like the 'new gal' anymore, this label was consistently re-mentioned as they met me for the first time. I couldn't wait to get involved, as if you hadn't been to Iraq, you didn't understand half of the chat that went on at socials and over a brew in the tea bar. They would talk about landing sites and bits of kit that I had never heard of. I was scheduled to go that August and I was beyond excited. That's the weird thing about so many of us in the forces. We look forward to deploying to war as that is ultimately what we joined up for. Flying around the UK is fun, but unless someone is relying on you to move them, their ammunition, rations, or kit it doesn't really make a difference to anyone's life.

I deployed to Basra in Iraq in August 2003 aged 21 and was still Limited Combat Ready. I was, I believe the youngest aircrew ever to deploy to the front line, I was still LCR, and my Iraq medal had 'Aircrew Cadet' written on it, which at the time was unique. The main war-fighting part of the conflict was over by the time I arrived, so we were flying what was called 'framework tasking' and holding IRT (Immediate Response Team) or flying ambulance from a base called Al Amara, halfway up the country. The tasking entailed a daily round robin of the Forward Operating Bases (FOB) with troops on board and bits of kit to deliver. I guess it was similar to the Falklands, but a lot warmer; like a whole lot warmer. Now being from Northern Ireland this hit me like a wall. It was about 38–40 Celsius out there and you had to respect the heat or it could kill you. On my second day, we had to go to the range and check fire our rifles. I watched as one of our engineers nearly died with heat stroke and had to be medevacked to the field hospital at Shaibar. It zaps your energy, so any task feels so much harder, then add body armour and a flying helmet. But as expected, I loved it and it was weight-loss island! Bonus.

On returning to the UK, I was pencilled in for my Combat Ready Check that October. Now they say that all the best people fail their first CR check, and I can indeed confirm this. I crashed and burned in a sea of nerves from the second we took off on that check ride, messing up my checks and talking all over radio calls with my over-enthusiasm to show I knew what the tasking was. It went from bad to worse when I ran off the aircraft to go to the portaloo at one point while we were sitting on the ground awaiting the arrival of our troops. As I ran in, and the plastic door swung closed behind me I found myself in the only portaloo out of fifty scattered around the exercise area on Salisbury Plain that one of our crews had blown over the previous day. Every single surface was covered in the contents of the unlucky capsule. Trying not to barf, I gingerly pushed the door back open with my foot and managed to extract myself without any part of my body touching any part of the decorated walls. The worst bit, however, was that we were on an exercise at the time called 'Eagles Eye'. This involved us flying 16 Air Assault Brigade the length of the country to assault Kildare Forest in Scotland and then setting up camp in a very soggy and grim West Freugh, or 'Wet Through' as we lovingly referred to it. Because it was a combined exercise with the Chinook fleet, Pumas and Merlins there were lots of people I knew knocking around. Therefore, they all knew when the day came for my CR check. I knew by the time we landed I had failed it, but we had to go to the debrief in the corner of the hangar for the news to be delivered. Then the worst bit was having to walk back through the hangar to where all the aircrew were sitting on their cot beds, having to inform everyone who eagerly asked as I walked past, that I had 'flunked' it. A few weeks later, however, I was given my second attempt. This was out in Bruggen, Germany doing some USLs for a course of soldiers. We flew out to Bruggen, serviced the aircraft then went out for a few drinks. I was being very careful not to drink much, as the check was in the morning. My crewmate Mick Fry bought himself and Craig, the standards guy doing my check ride, drinks all night. He was far more drunk than the rest of us by a country mile. Turns out Mick had been adding vodka to his pints. The next morning, we crewed in, picked up our first USL and flew a circuit back to the runway. Craig announced that I had passed, and could we land so he could get off. Mick and I flew the rest of the day with lots of giggles. He absolutely knew what he was doing that night and poor Craig was reaping the benefits of Mick's secret plan. That evening we all went out to celebrate and this time I wasn't allowed to buy a single drink. This was not a good thing as it turned out, and German yellow sherbet vodka has a lot to answer for, as does my crewmate Fryster. The long walk back to our accommodation from the main gate at Bruggen in November nearly gave me hypothermia – it took that long to stagger …

So now fully Combat Ready, in January 2005 I headed out to Iraq again for my second time. This time, as I had made the grade, I was allowed to be crewed up with another CR crewman and one of my best mates, Logie. It was so nice to be flying without the eyes of an instructor on me and just enjoy it properly for the first time. They say you only really learn how to drive after you pass your test, and this can be said for crewman life. When there is no 'adult' around to ask questions of, you have to make choices for yourself, but at least you always have another crewman to split the decision with and indeed the subsequent blame if it all goes wrong! Logie and I had the best crew with JP and JB as pilots. Not confusing on the intercom at all. JP was one of the safest set of hands on the squadron and JB had been on my Shawbury Course and was already a great friend. We used to routinely carry out a task called Eagle VCPs which is short for Vehicle Check points. This would entail us dropping some RAF regiment troops off at random locations on the highway, then flying off for fifteen to twenty minutes while they did vehicle searches for anything suspicious, mostly weapons. We had a blast filling those twenty minutes each time, doing stunts around the sky. JP, rightly so, wanted to show JB what the aircraft 'could' do but in a safe way and with supervision, so he then had the skill set to get out of trouble if ever needed. We practised 'Gornies', which were basically corkscrews upwards then tipping the nose over and flying into fresh air to depart the manoeuvre; Quick Stops, a dynamic manoeuvre going from maximum speed to land on a penny, as if you had a late spot on your troops or landing site and needed to get in; and my favourite of all 'bunting'. Now 'bunting' is not what you would call a 'recognised technique' in the manual of helicopter flying. It basically involves the pilot climbing the aircraft to a safe height above the ground then dumping the collective lever rapidly so the whole aircraft effectively goes 'weightless'. When the cockpit called a 'bunt', 'bunt go' on the intercom, fun and chaos ensued in the cabin. From doing loops through the restraint straps we had attached to the roof and seeing how many rolls we could get in, to flying the length of the aircraft on the 'broomstick', sorry brush, that we carried behind the step ladder! Pre-'bunt' we ensured all kit was thoroughly strapped down to the floor and that anyone on board knew what was coming and tightened or 'loosened' their seat belts slightly depending on their boisterousness. The post 'bunt' clear up was always fun though. Looking around the cabin to see a mix of ear-to-ear grins or ear-to-ear fear amongst some and of course the odd one ear-to-ear in vomit. Carefully, we put anything that had freed itself from its bondage back under the seats, or indeed very, very, slowly reeled in the long belt of 7.62 that had made a break for freedom out of the ramp's M60 and was now precariously flapping in the wind, not my favourite moment (ha-ha). It wasn't just the things in the cabin that got airborne from where they should be, most of the oil in the aircraft transmissions did the same. The engineers would open the maintenance panels to do a post-flight servicing to be met with a wash of oil spread on every surface. They would try and hide their jealousy in their eye rolling and head shaking while stifling a smile, 'have you been bunting' … NOOOOOO came the answer, 'just some turbulence' …

My more memorable moments of our 'stunt' flying/time filling during EVCPs was for all the wrong reasons. In Iraq there were large water pipes to provide irrigation around the area surrounding Basra. They would routinely burst, resulting in 50–60ft high fountains spraying upwards into the air. Now bearing in mind it was 40+ degrees Celsius, one day JP suggested we fly through one of the fountains to cool off, as we in the cabin could bathe in the cool water as it came into the front door and ramp. Great plan, let's do it! And it was, until mid-fountain we realised it was a sewer pipe that had burst. Doh. Iraq was definitely a good way to start my introduction to war. The tasking was relaxed, and the pace of life was easy. I remember my wisdom teeth becoming sore with an infection and jumping off the aircraft at Shaibar to get them looked at by the dentist. The other crewman took his time to load a vehicle into the cabin of the aircraft while it was shut down. Then I jumped back on board, after having my teeth injected, to carry on tasking. Something that would never be allowed in today's climate.

One morning we were tasked to take a lot of troops out to the range to check fire their rifles again, which was common practice. We landed at Diamond Back range and offloaded a cabin full of troops. While Logie and I were 'heads in', tidying up the cabin and seat belts our pilot JP piped up on the intercom. 'Who the fuck is that bearded twat walking under our disc in the 2 o'clock?' Now with Chinooks we are very careful with clearing people in and out of the safety area around the rotor discs as they can clearly kill people. But this guy had just decided not to bother waiting for a thumbs up. He had a short dark beard and was wearing some kit that wasn't the norm for our other troops, so we all guessed he was 'Special Forces'. He asked for a headset which we provided and when he was able to talk on the intercom asked if we could give him and a few mates a lift back to Basra which was only ten minutes flying. We had no other tasking to do so we said yes. Now I was still reeling from him approaching the aircraft without me giving him a thumbs up, so was being a little less happy and smiley than I normally would be. I wanted them to know they had done wrong but hadn't got the guts to tell them. When we landed and they got off the aircraft I sent Logie off to have a word with them while I did the refuel. They may be 'Special', but it was my job to control the aircraft and passengers' safety. I am sure Logie laughed while disconnecting his comms lead 'yes Liz' as he jumped off to go have a smoke for a few minutes.

Later that night we were running the 'Camel's Toe Bar' at Basra, a bar we had built for the camp where you could go and enjoy your daily two cans of beer with a beer token chit we had been issued. The bar was huge, we had managed to get a T54 tank in there, a few palm trees, and some Astro turf and tables. We also 'acquired' a local's canoe but that's a story for the bar sometime. Most of the sections took turns to run the Camel's Toe and that night myself and a few other crewmen were the nominated bar staff. I looked up at one point of the evening and who should I see walking up to the bar but the same bearded 'Special Forces' guy. I handed him his two beers and while marking up his beer chit with my pen, I casually said 'So you got home alright today then?' He looked up at me and grinned … 'Ah, you're that angry lesbian off the back of the Chinook, aren't you?' (I didn't even have short hair anymore and I was still being called this, the irony was not wasted.) The man staring back at me would occupy the rest of my life as a crewman.

Chapter 6

Doris

So, for the second half of my deployment in Iraq I spent most of my spare time with Skelfy. Now don't get me wrong, Basra was certainly not a place for dating or in fact public signs of affection, but we caught up for drinks in the Camel's Toe bar again, chatted at the gym and went to the NAAFI shop on base for Magnum ice creams on the odd afternoon I wasn't flying. We would go out for pizzas from the Pizza Hut on camp. That's the thing with big bases when you are deployed, usually there are a few creature comforts such as Pizza Hut or Burger King to try and make you feel slightly more at home. So, I guess looking back, all in all it was quite romantic. One thing was for sure, my 23-year-old self was smitten. Unfortunately for me, however, the rest of the crewmen were not so taken with my new partner in crime and eyeballed him with an element of suspicion. I was their gal, it was almost as though they owned me but in a rather sweet way, and any potential suitor had to make the grade. They used to take the micky out of me in the evening as I got ready, or as 'ready' as you can in cargo pants and a T-shirt. But I had a tiny little bottle of perfume with me, no make-up or hairdryer just a teeny, tiny, bottle of Ghost. I'd dab a little on every night before checking myself in the postcard-sized mirror I had balanced on one of the levels of my fabric hanging shelves. The odd time, Skelfy would even call round for me. I always saw this as an opportunity to introduce the lads to him properly. This didn't really help as Skelfy was indeed 'Special Forces' or SF as we called them. As such, he was a very dominating Alpha-male character who did not do much in terms of small talk to win them over.

DORIS

After a while, the lads I shared a tent with began a series of well-intended pranks at my expense. In the evenings, I would stay out as late as was reasonably possible over at Skelfy's tent, then sneak back into mine around midnight and try not to wake the guys who were already sleeping. I thought mostly I had got away without them caring much. However, a few weeks into my little routine of quietly unzipping the main door into our big main tent pod then sliding in towards my little single sleeping pod that was just inside on the left, easy to get to, or so I thought, something was amiss. I felt around in the dark, trying to locate the zip of the netted fabric to allow me into my little pod where my cot bed was located but found nothing, the zip had gone. In the darkened room it took me ages to work out what had happened. They had rotated my pod 180 degrees, so the zip access door was now neatly flat against the wall of the tent. This meant the side I was feeling up for the entrance was just a sheer panel of net. I had to do my best spiderwoman impersonation to climb over and around my pod to manoeuvre into my cot bed. Very amusing lads, well done.

A few nights later, I was just leaving the tent as the lads were forming a chain to lug boxes of water into the hallway next to the fridge. Never one to shirk my duty I stopped to give a hand until we had emptied the wagon of sixty-plus boxes of bottled water, then headed out for my 'date'. This time on returning, as I slowly unzipped the main door to keep the noise down, there was a strange glow coming from inside the door. I tiptoed in to be faced with a wall of water boxes that had been constructed into an igloo around my little bed pod, all the way to the ceiling. And what's more they had helpfully stuck cylumes (glow sticks) on the boxes to showcase their amazing creation in the dark for me. Awesome. So I began to remove the box bricks just enough to make a little entrance hole to clamber in through, while swearing lots and actually trying not to laugh. This didn't matter though as in the darkness I began to hear the sniggering from the little cot beds around the tent. Not only had I helped them move the boxes for my own undoing, but they made a little video of them building the igloo to show me the next day. Wankers.

The final straw came a week later when I came back in the middle of the night. As I was slowly undoing the zip on the main door, I noticed the A4 sheet of paper in the polly pocket stuck to the front of the door panel had changed. It was usually a layout with all our names on the spaces where we slept so people could find us if they needed to wake us in an emergency. Where my bed space was it read 'TV and Sitting Area'. You are kidding me. I went in and found my little safe space, where all my stuff used to sit in my little pod – what I called home – was gone. In its place was our widescreen TV and some camping chairs. I flashed. This is the term we use when you absolutely have had enough! The lights went on, the air turned blue, and I huffed as I climbed into one of the empty beds we had! The next morning, they helped me put it all back together, but I wouldn't speak at all. This was how they knew they had crossed the line as I never normally shut up. I must admit though, they did surpass themselves that night; it still makes me chuckle …

As the weeks went on, they did eventually grow to like Skelfy, mainly as he seemed to have an endless supply of spare beer tokens and also had his own wagon. One night he offered to take us up to the other bar on camp which was a little too far for us to walk to. We all crammed into his hi-lux, I think we squeezed thirteen of us in which was a new record, and off we headed up to the 'commanders' bar'. This bar was indoors, unlike the Camel's Toe, and had some really long right-angled Iraq-style sofas in it. I took a seat and the other Chinny boys sat down between myself and Skelfy. It was hilarious, as every time Skelfy wanted to get me a beer, he had to ask the lad next to him, 'Ask Liz if she wants a drink.' This would then get rippled along to me, and then the reply of 'Yes, Strongbow please' would get passed back along the line. It was like one of those Asian date nights and quite amusing looking back. I still remember sharing our first kiss against the HESCO Bastion wall outside the back of his tent. HESCO are huge, matted containers, kept together by a mesh of wire and filled with sand. They are what the forces have used as blast defences in recent years and of course one of the reasons why Bastion in Helmand got its name. So, there I was in the dark, in a war zone, in my combats, pressed up against a blast wall, slowly falling in love. Not quite Romeo and Juliet but it was simple, and it was real.

The detachment eventually came to an end and it was time for me to say goodbye to Skelfy. I did not want to come home, I had fallen so badly and if I'm honest I wasn't sure that I would ever actually see him again. Skelfy was staying in Basra for a few more weeks so we kept in touch when I got back to the UK via MSN messenger (as it was in those days before Facebook and Instagram existed). One night we had a lovely long chat and I missed him so much when he signed off. I headed to bed in my little room in the sergeants' mess only to be woken up with a start at 4 a.m. ... there was someone standing in my room. In the twilight haze it took a few seconds for my eyes to focus properly on the intruder's silhouette. It was him! He had been messaging me from the halfway point on his return journey home to the UK but hadn't let on! On landing he had driven straight from RAF Brize Norton to RAF Odiham, found an open window to climb into the sergeants' mess, found reception and tracked down which room I was in. I never locked my door when I lived in the mess as it was as safe as houses and I get up about a billion times to pee every night, the toilets being down the corridor. But there he was, in the flesh in the UK, not just a Basra romance. The perks of dating someone from the SAS is they can do these types of surprises when you are least expecting it! The only disappointing bit was he hadn't brought any Milk Tray.

Now that we were both back in the UK it was time for Skelfy to meet my 'best' crewmates. We were all thick as thieves, mostly due to circumstances that we all lived in the mess together, spending most weekends getting drunk in the bar for peanuts. Grohly, Burnsy, Bob and I made up a great little fourship. They were all older than me and again were like big brothers, so their approval meant a lot to me. These three also all happened to now work on 7 Squadron who flew the 'SF' boys around and worked closely with them on deployments. This made for an easy introduction as they knew a lot of Skelfy's mates already. I remember the first time he met Burnsy and Fryster on a night out in Basingstoke, the nearest big town to camp. We joined them after dinner in Chicago's at the top of town, incidentally the best cheesy rock bar EVER. I still miss those nights playing the air guitar on the dance floor to Bon Jovi's *Living on a Prayer* and my favourite rock dance move: the reach and grab. Ask me when we meet, and I'll show you sometime! Anyway, on arrival I nipped off to the ladies and when I came back minutes later, they were already best buddies. I was nearly surplus to requirements. Skelfy told me in the taxi home later that night that Fryster had said to him earlier in the evening 'I don't care how special you are, that's our girl, don't mess her about.' And then they shook hands, and all was good: gentleman to gentleman.

Over the next few years, Burnsy and I shared a house that the RAF had rented for us, so he and Skelfy got to know each other pretty well. We had all been offered the chance to move off camp as they were running out of rooms in the mess. I had asked to be paired with Logie at the time as he was easy going, a really great mate and we were on the same wavelength. However, I returned from one of my Morocco deployments to discover they had paired me up with Burnsy. I knew Burnsy well as he was one of the fourship, but we were like chalk and cheese. He was into hunting and fishing, making casseroles with bits of animal bones sticking out and watched *Countryfile* and wildlife programmes on TV, while I was into fashion, lived on salads due to my lack of cooking skills and watched *Sex and the City* and *Friends*. We were opposite ends of the spectrum, but oh my word it worked! We had an absolute blast living together, he taught me how to cook and I taught him that vertical stripes are more slimming for the figure than horizontal ones. I still remember the first night he was night flying and I cooked for myself. I rang Burnsy to tell him and he was very impressed! 'What did you make?' he asked. 'Corn on the cob' came my reply. He tried not to laugh, but I think he was just impressed that I hadn't 'burnt water' or indeed our house down. One of my fondest memories of my time living with Burnsy was a night out for Grohly's birthday. The three of us headed out into Basingstoke, our nearest town, and got extremely drunk. When Burnsy and I got home we made the mistake of pouring another glass of red and putting some music on. I came down the stairs the following morning and instantly thought we had been burgled. The front door was slightly open, and I walked into the conservatory to be greeted by a sea of CD cases sprawled across the conservatory floor and the double-glazed doors to the garden wide open. Then my memory kicked in, we hadn't been burgled at all, Burnsy had wanted to find some Pink Floyd CD that was in the wrong case, and I had just been too drunk to close the bloody front door behind us on arriving home. Meanwhile, Burnsy went for a smoke in the garden and left the conservatory doors open behind him too!

Those early days of Skelfy and I were certainly not plain sailing though. He was away a lot, as was I, and we had a few break-ups to say the least. Burnsy was there with the cups of tea and tissues every time bless him, scooping my ass off the floor. One night, as Skelfy and I were walking back from our local, we chanced upon a Sainsbury's trolley that had been abandoned at the side of the path. What luck, transport home! I jumped in and Skelfy pushed me the whole way back, we laughed so hard trying not to crash. When we got home, we were still giggling away, Burnsy was already tucked up in bed upstairs. He came down the next morning to find our newly acquired trolley parked in the centre of the kitchen. That trolley turned out to make the best bar trolley for our BBQs and parties over the years with a plastic box full of ice set in it and all the mixers stashed underneath! Our pure genius took some explaining to the landlord when he visited though!

Throughout these good times, Skelfy began to refer to me as 'Doris'. This is a term used in the military for females. It is not derogatory, as you may think, but a term of endearment. Women throughout the forces since the Second World War have been referred to as 'Doris'. But the important thing for me was when the rest of the lads started calling me 'Doris' as well. It meant that they thought enough of me to call me it to my face, knowing I wouldn't throw my arms up in offence. It was like a seal of approval. So over time, once my crew mates began to call me Doris, the name caught on. Eventually, the entire squadron referred to me as 'Doris' and I had it on my squadron mug, and even my email signature. I was proud to be Doris. I was the only Doris crewman at Odiham at the time and I loved it. After a few years when we got some more female crewmen on the Chinook fleet, I was still Doris number one. They were all allocated 'Doris' numbers thereafter but it never quite caught on with them as much as it stuck with me. A few years later, the first time I took Skelfy home to meet my parents, we were all sitting in the dining room when Skelfy said, 'Doris, pop the kettle on and make us a brew,' at which my mum's eyeballs nearly fell out of her head. She never even called me 'Liz', as my name was Elizabeth. She always used it in full. Her immediate response was 'Doris? Who is Doris?' To which Skelfy replied 'Liz.' That wasn't much better in her eyes. I used to get Skelfy to call me it as much as possible in her company just to wind her up. Sorry Mum.

The end of the Chinooks' involvement in Iraq came in April 2005 when we handed over to the Merlin fleet. This was their first proper deployment since coming into service and they would be taking over the routine tasking duties that the Chinook force had been doing since the invasion in 2003, which incidentally I had watched on a TV from the crew room on 60 Squadron at Shawbury while in training. As I mentioned previously there was always lots of rivalry between helicopter fleets but especially so between us and the Merlins for some reason. Maybe it's because the Pumas knew they were not a Chinook, and they had carved out a role for themselves in delivering the Special Forces chaps to rooftops. The Merlins, however, thought they were as capable as Chinooks, which wound us up a treat as they were not in our league payload- and performance-wise. I was on the aircraft that was tasked to fly south from Basra to meet the first Merlins coming into country at the port of Um Qasar. Once we had them on frequency there was instant banter along the lines of 'nice of you to finally show up' etc. Now, on landing at any base the first check we do is 'arm down' the defence systems so that they do not trigger on the ground from the radars and weapons at the base. It's essential to do this; if you don't you could potentially fire the decoy flares that we have fitted to the aircraft, and, if you're unlucky, hit one of the ground crew or awaiting passengers. As we taxied in with the Merlins following behind us, I looked out of the ramp and saw the first Merlin to land at Basra airbase fire its flares out all over the dispersal. Once again, our captain piped up on the radio 'Did someone book a fireworks display?' as we all chuckled to ourselves.

I will always look back at my time in Iraq with the fondest of memories. For what was considered a war zone, this place gave me some of my favourite stories. I was young, doing the job I had joined to do and had very few cares in the world. The IRT wasn't that busy, so we didn't see much in terms of injuries or gore and my time holding that duty was mainly spent watching the Series *24* back-to-back with my mates or signing our names on the brick wall of the building. In fact, during my time there I was lucky enough to be mostly shielded from the raw face of death and the carnage of war. Sadly, however, I did witness the consequences of a flying accident for the first time in my career. One of the other RAF helicopters operating in theatre was the Puma. They mainly flew from Bagdad but had the odd crew and aircraft down with us in Basra. We got to know the Puma crews fairly well as they rotated through and joined us in the Camel's Toe for a beer. One morning, one of their aircraft crashed when coming into land at Basra. Some of our crews saw it happen from the flight line, the rest of us just heard it and saw the billowing smoke. The co-pilot, Kris, didn't make it out of the burning wreckage, however, the pilot and crewman were loaded on to one of our aircraft to be taken to the hospital at Shaibar. I remember that night Stu and Roly telling us they could hear their screams over the noise of the aircraft; they had been burnt so badly. That stayed with me for the rest of my career. We had the best job in the world in my opinion and got paid handsomely for it. But when it goes wrong in a helicopter, it goes spectacularly wrong, and very quickly. You can never be off your game or distracted in the air as the result can be fatal. I realised that day that it wasn't always the enemy that would be out to kill me but that the ground also had a probable kill (PK) of one.

Above: Graham and me –
Christmas Kids and that ghastly
orange sofa

Right: The 'Aircrew Wall of
Fame' at Al Amara, Iraq – we all
made a brick; I'm the Golden
Arches!

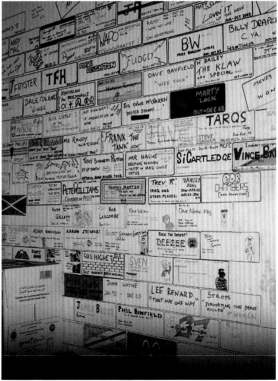

Beautiful Kajaki Dam, top of the Helmand Valley

Landing in the red desert Afghanistan – there's a Chinook in there somewhere …

Wire strike damage, from Kajaki Dam

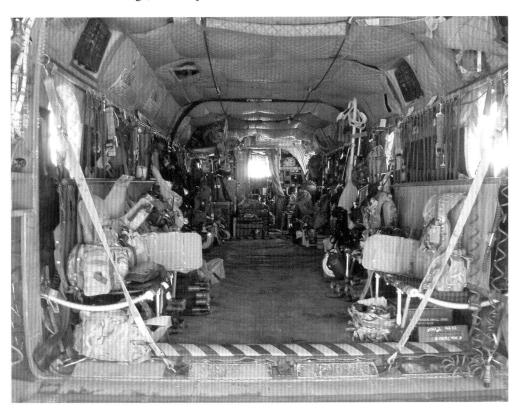

MERT cab with its rubber mat flooring

Left: 'The' coat

Below: Stretchers coming towards the ramp on MERT

Above left: IRT blast wall with 'Tricky 73', the MERT aircraft callsign

Above right: 1310 Flt wall, taken just before we left theatre for good back in 2014

Above: Odiham High Street blast wall art – there's no place like home!

Right: Anna and me

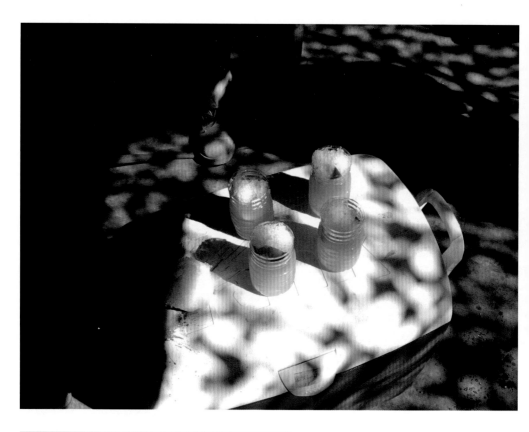

Above: Ramp cocktails in Morocco with Atlas mountains ice and snowball fights!

Left: The view from the top of the aircraft on HMS *Ocean*

My drags at the urinals

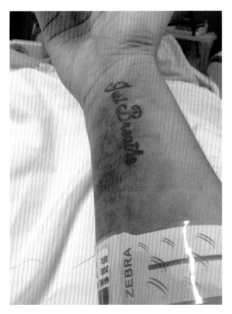

Above left: Just Breathe … words to live by but easier said than done sometimes

Above right: My poppy bouquet with my old combat material binding the handle

Above: The Aerobility Team visiting RAF Odiham and my beloved Chinook

Left: The best of times and the worst of times, but I would do it all again in an instant

Chapter 7

Hello Helmand

In 2005, after withdrawing from Iraq, the Chinook force turned their eyes towards Afghanistan. There was one mandatory course we all had to complete before any aircrew could deploy to Op Herrick. This was the infamous Escape and Evasion course, the 'A' course. It was well known to be the most horrendous course we would ever have to do, but it was to prepare us for the worst if we were ever to get captured by the enemy, in particular the Taliban. It was a two-week course, on which we would go on the run from a hunter force until we got caught or 'bounced' as we called it. All you would be wearing was your flying suit and a flying jacket. This was done to mimic you being in a downed aircraft behind enemy lines with no other kit than what you are wearing. We all tried to smuggle things with us to help us on the run, I even went to the lengths of stitching Curly Wurly bars into the lining of my jacket, but the staff search you before they send you off on to the exercise area and sadly all my contraband was found, but I got an A star for effort. My course fell in January; thus, I spent the coldest week of my life on the run with a teammate, sleeping in bushes and ditches by day and moving across fields under the cover of darkness at night. By the time you are caught you are cold, hungry and tired and usually wet. To be honest, by then you are quite thankful to be screamed at, thrown in a puddle face down and hooded, as you knew the truck you were about to be loaded into may provide some shelter. We were then taken off to what we referred to as the 'monkey' house which was the 'resistance to interrogation' building located at RAF St Mawgan and is a horrible, soulless concrete bunker.

Once offloaded and processed we would be put through a series of interrogation interviews while being conditioned to breaking point or 'point of duress'. The point of duress was when you had no option but to start talking, i.e. a weapon was shoved in the side of your head or mouth, and part of the course was gauging this point for yourself. Up until the point of duress you were to only tell the interrogators your name, rank and number and slowly drip-feed any information that wasn't secret. It was very similar to what the SAS *Who Dares Wins* programme has demonstrated as they gleefully destroy minor celebrities on it. The conditioning, however, was the ruthless bit, as this was a way of breaking down recruits so we would get too fatigued to hold our nerve and tongues. The conditioning came in the form of white noise, stress positions and being subjected to the recorded sound of a baby crying relentlessly. All the while wearing a hood over your head, covering your face and your wrists tie-wrapped together. We were locked in tiny cages and made to do thankless tasks, such as moving a puddle around a hangar with a spoon! It sounds inhumane, but it is designed to mimic how you may be treated if caught by an enemy and trust me I would rather be prepped with training if this were to ever happen than deal with this scenario without training. It's designed to disorientate you, so you lose track of time and your bearings. I kept my mind engaged by mentally going through my wardrobe in my head and matching my shoes to my outfits. Sounds ridiculous but it worked and keeping your mind focused and occupied is a well-known strategy to survive captivity. There is one famous story of a captive who built a hotel in his head – all the way from designing and building it to the staff employed, internal décor, and menu! The initial conditioning was followed by a strip search then into the interrogations. During my first strip search, they ripped off the tape I had put over my ankles before we went on the run. The only way I knew I was in the same room during my second strip search a week later, was that I saw my tape lurking in the corner of this bland concrete room. These little wins become mental victories as it is very much a battle of you versus the interrogation staff. The more you can keep your bearings and your head together the longer you will last.

By far the worst memory from my course was during one of my interrogations. Now weirdly you came to enjoy being taken for your interrogations as, to be honest, by that point anything was better than stress positions, with your hands placed on your head or pressed against an ice-cold wall. But one interrogation remains gruesomely etched in my mind. After the strip search, all we were permitted to put back on were our pants, flying suit and boots. No socks, no sports bra, no dignity. All you could hope for was that the zip on your flying suit remained intact and didn't flail open as was sometimes the case. On this particular interrogation session, the man screaming at me in a balaclava got closer and closer into my face. He was so close and screaming so hard that some of his saliva exploded from his mouth and landed on my chest. Hands tied together there was little I could do about this. However, to add insult to injury this blob of saliva began to make its way down my chest. Now as if this wasn't bad enough, had I been wearing a sports bra it would have at least stopped at that damn point. But oh no, it continued to roll down my chest and all the way to my belly button. Still makes me cringe now thinking about it, but at least it distracted me from the screaming. I was also unlucky enough to be put on a course starting 5 January, which meant going on the run and freezing my ass off on Bodmin Moor in Devon with just a flying suit and jacket to wear. No food for days and surviving on adrenaline. It was the hardest thing I have ever done but it changes who you are and shows you just how strong your mind can be when it is the only thing within your control. Giving up on this course was not an option as I would never put myself through it again. I finished the course with infected blisters on my ankles that were so bad I couldn't wear shoes for two weeks and a cold weather injury for the rest of my life, but I passed it.

I was now all set to deploy on Operation Herrick with 27 Squadron A Flight in March 2006. During the early days for the British military in Afghanistan, Camp Bastion didn't exist, so we flew and operated from Kandahar Airbase or KAF as we called it. This was a huge American-run base and had a great set up. There was a place called the boardwalk in the centre of the camp with a recreation area in the middle. It was surrounded by a few coffee shops in the form of a Tim Horton's and The Green Bean, along with a Pizza Hut, Subway and Burger King. It was where we spent most of our days when we had some time to chill and weren't flying. The other place I frequented most was the massive American gym. This was a great place to wash off an afternoon rather than just sitting in my room, and probably when I started to really get into my running. Running became my decompression time and as the years went on, I ran more and more as I had so much to empty out of my brain at the end of a day in a war zone. I even got quite good at it as the weight dropped off me! The Americans went to war very well, even the food hall was massive and had everything you could ever want on tap, pretty much 24/7. Our crews used to fill their pockets with as many goodies as they could fit every time we went in, from Snickers ice creams to packets of Jolly Ranchers and protein bars. We must have looked like homeless people as we gathered them up by the handful and stuffed our pockets to bursting point. They also had 'surf and turf' nights where the massive steaks on the servery were bigger than my head. If I'm honest this still didn't really feel like a war zone. The only downside of the whole set up was that we were put in an accommodation block next to the camp's main sewage plant or the 'poo pond' as we 'not' so affectionately called it. This mostly surfaced as a problem every evening when the wind direction changed from easterly to westerly and the familiar smell of human excrement now wafted over our accommodation. Some nights it was worse than ever, and the ongoing joke was 'how much would it take for you to swim the poo pond?' There was a rumour that a Romanian soldier had actually tried this and subsequently died from the fumes he inhaled – or so the urban myth went. What a way to go eh? Suffocated by shit. There wasn't enough money in the world for me to try that, but some people's low cash threshold did surprise me!

As I mentioned earlier, Camp Bastion was yet to be built and that's where the Chinook force came into its own. Our main task on the very early Op Herricks was to under sling huge ISO containers full of building kit west from KAF to the site where Bastion was being constructed. This was about an hour's flying across the 'red desert' which was the most awesome span of rippling red sand I have ever seen, and it stretched out for miles. The most distinctive thing about it was the edges of it, where it literally just stopped, and the sand became a normal beige colour. It didn't fade out in colour or gradually change; it was like thick red granular icing poured on a cake that just hardened at the edge. I've often been asked if I ever wanted to be a pilot and the truth is no, I had the best seat in the house sitting on that ramp with my harness attached, legs dangling out watching the world go by, both in the UK and abroad. This transit was sometimes fairly mundane with little to see so we always used to play 'in crew' games such as *Desert Island Discs* choices (for the record, mine was the Eagles *Greatest Hits*) or ponder 'would you rather fight a blind tiger or a lion with three legs?' and variations on this theme. We also played our very own unique version of 'Marry, Snog, Avoid' regarding females whom we knew or were famous. Being the only female on most crews I was expected to give my answer regardless of the fact that I am NOT a lesbian. I was also not naïve enough to think that my name had not come up during this game on many other crews' aircraft over the years and all I can hope for looking back is that I was one of the first two options! We made up plenty of games to fill our time and got to know one another scarily well over the span of a three-month deployment. Fortunately, the cockpit voice recorder only has a twenty-minute loop as many of these discussions I will take to the grave and thank God no one else heard most of them ...

During this laborious sixty-minute transit across the desert you were unlikely to see much in terms of civilisation except the odd

Bedouin camp. What did always strike me as odd, however, was every so often we would see a man walking. A lone figure, miles from anywhere. I always wondered what was so important that they would endure this lonely pilgrimage in the crippling Afghan heat and if they knew how far it was to the next point of human contact? This only confirmed what I already knew. The Afghan people are the hardiest people on earth, and unfortunately for us so were the Taliban.

My favourite moment of every tasking day was to lower the ramp so it was level, and watch the sun set behind us as we flew east across the red desert, our work for the day safely finished and heading home. Sitting on the ramp you could feel the lovely warm air from the engine exhausts being sucked back into the cabin, you were over safe territory in the red desert and high enough to avoid the altitude height that most bullets could climb to. I adored being able to just zone out while watching the sun slip away like a gold coin, signifying another day over, and another day closer to heading back to my Skelfy.

Once Bastion started to take shape in the form of a barbed wire fence and a few tents and rows of HESCO Bastion we deployed two of our crews to spend a week at a time based from there, holding IRT. This was the 'Immediate Response Team' similar to Iraq and now that we had British boots on the ground in the Southern Helmand it was essential that we held a 'readiness crew' of medics and an aircraft to go and get anyone who became injured. These early days at Bastion where the best, as there were so few people around you were left to get on with your job without being bothered too much. We even had the odd BBQ, but rather hilariously these were built with wooden pallets. The challenge was to try and cook the massive steaks that our opposite crews pinched from the cook house at KAF and brought across to Bastion in a cooler box, before the structure itself burnt to the ground. We lived in a 12ft-by-12ft military tent, with no air conditioning, sleeping on sweaty little green cot beds and we shared a joint shower tent with the Paras at the time. This was not common practice may I add, but the infrastructure was so limited we had to. Each morning I would head down with one of the crewmen who would kindly offer to guard the curtain for me. By 'the curtain' I am referring to the only curtain in a row of metal showers that looked like a cattle milking area. The first morning I walked in, there were a row of Paras all brushing their teeth in their boxer shorts and towels. I climbed in behind 'the curtain', wriggled out of my clothes, hung them up so they didn't get wet – they always did – showered then dressed and out. By the time I re-emerged minutes later, each and every one of them were stark naked still brushing their teeth. I laughed and rolled my eyes, which signalled that I had a sense of humour, and they knew it was game on thereafter. Every morning I would walk in to their greeting of 'Morning ma'am', only to walk out from my curtain to a row of naked bums. No need to complain I thought to myself ...

These early days flying around Southern Helmand and holding IRT were still fairly benign. Our usual days tasking consisted of a 'round robin' visiting the three main Forward Operating Bases (FOBs). These at that time were FOB Sangin, FOB Price and Lashkar Gah which was in the middle of a town just south-east of Bastion. We had the odd transit way up north to another of our FOBs and the most beautiful place, Kajaki Dam. It was so picturesque up there as the site was obviously located by a huge lake, the main water supply for the Helmand Valley. The water was the purest sparkling, crystal-clear blue and always looked so inviting from a hot dusty aircraft. On top of this, the forty-five minutes it took to fly up there was over some of the most amazing mountain ranges I have ever seen. This was by far my favourite place to fly to in Helmand. Afghanistan is the most stunning country I have flown over; it is such a shame it has been plagued by fighting for hundreds of years. Maybe that's why it has maintained its raw beauty, as it has never become a holiday destination and so much of its topography remains untouched by western cosmetics.

We would be briefed with daily intelligence updates about the Taliban threat in the Helmand Valley, but the golden rule was to avoid the 'Green Zone'. This was a strip of green, fertile, cropped land that ran north to south down the middle of the Valley astride the river. It was so lush and green as the Afghans have a very clever irrigation system in place to utilise their limited water supply. The Green Zone was where most of the population lived and grew their crops to live off. This is also where the Taliban lived and grew THEIR crops of weapons.

But the most valuable crop grown in the Green Zone by far were the endless fields of poppies. These were fiercely protected by both the Taliban and the local farmers because this is what brought in the money. The harvesting of the poppy fields consisted of them being set alight and then the scorched pods being cut open to reveal their prize: raw opium sap. This would then be dried to make opiate powder before being refined into the heroin that we see demolishing lives on UK soil. You can't really blame the farmers, who grew this valuable crop, for shooting at us every time we came near, and oh my they did. It was their livelihood that was under threat, and along with that their family, so the odd potshot at us as we flew past was justified in their eyes. Speaking of which, even with your eyes closed you could smell when you were in the Green Zone, it had such a unique aroma in contrast to the arid desert. It smelt like a botanical garden but with a dry edge to it. That smell always equalled bullets nearly every time, but it also meant some of the fastest, lowest, most exciting flying we ever did. 'Gotta take the good with the bad' as they say!

It was our responsibility to man the weapons fitted to the aircraft, and with that came the responsibility of the decision when to press or pull the trigger. In Iraq we only flew with an M60 fitted on the ramp and in the right-hand door. I say 'only', it still fired 7.62 but at around 100 rounds per minute and was indeed operated by pulling a conventional trigger. It was a trusty old weapon and as mentioned earlier had been used by the Huey crews in Vietnam and features heavily in lots of war movies from that conflict. However, Afghan was a different ball game altogether with a greater threat. We retained an M60 on the ramp mount so we could remove it easily if we needed to load vehicles inside, but we now had the impressive-looking miniguns to protect us. Not just the one; we had TWO fitted – one on each side at the front of the aircraft. These were a force of nature, firing 3,000 rounds per minute of 7.62 at the press of a little button. These weapons of mass destruction gave us the ability to protect our aircraft from all directions, sometimes without even needing to fire a bullet, the sight of them being enough of a deterrent to the enemy around. When you did, however, press that trigger you heard it spin up and basically within seconds anything you aimed at turned to mush. At night it looked like something out of a *Star Wars* film as the tracer rounds lit up the sky at maximum velocity, creating a straight orange line from weapon to target. When Op Herrick was at its most kinetic, we had very specific ROE (rules of engagement) numbered 492, which was escalated from purely self-defence ROE. Rule 492 allowed us to fire 'legally' on any suspected Taliban north of Highway One – the main transit road running east to west. Taliban were easily identifiable by the fact that they chose to wear black turbans which the locals did not. Now it would be easy to be blasé about this and fly around the province hosing baddies down, and don't get me wrong some US forces did, and did so legally. The problem with that plan, however, is when you pull the trigger of any weapon, even if you are within your right to do so, it is you who must live with the consequences for the rest of your life. With airborne weapons there is a term referred to as 'the separation of altitude'. This basically means you do not see the whites of people's eyes while you are shooting them, unlike close combat. I had weapons within my control to defend lives, not to take them. Of course, I had to use both the minigun and M60 at various times, especially for warning shots to keep the Taliban's heads down at a hot landing site to buy our troops cover to approach the aircraft. But any time I used it with pure lethal intent I was able to justify it with 'if it's him or me reasoning', i.e. if I do not squeeze the trigger right now, people on my aircraft will die. I know of others who took a slightly different more 'gung-ho' approach and were well within the Rules of Engagement to do so at the time. But I also know that some of their choices have come back to haunt them later in life. Having a weapon within your control, be it in the air or on the ground, demands a huge amount of respect. A respect for both the value of life and the finality of death.

It was ironic that during these early 'quieter' days I had my nearest death experience in a Chinook. Our crew were dropping off a USL at one of the drop points at Kajaki Dam. We set down the netted load in a cloud of dust and Logie swiftly released it from the centre hook. So far so good. As we transitioned away from the landing site, we flew directly into a massive set of high voltage wires. These were just like the ones you see here in the UK that we call 'helicopter killers'. The rotary fleet take a lot of caution with wires as we know how dangerous they are. We methodically study our maps before we fly to highlight them and always talk about them when navigating. This set of pylons, however, was not marked on any map. The first thing I remember was feeling the aircraft jolt with a loud bang, then seeing the wires spark off into the 3 o'clock of the aircraft. I was thrown into the metal frame of the front door and looked back to see Logie nearly go through the centre hatch as the aircraft lurched. He was saved from falling through by the safety harness we wear around our waists, attached to the airframe with a carabiner clip. The smell of burning electricity filled my nostrils – and I swear sometimes I can still smell that moment – as our Chinook started to tumble towards the ground. I thought for a second we had ripped our aft pylon off, which is basically the aft rotor head, as we were so out of control. The pilot shouted 'I can't see' as we got closer and closer to the ground. I knew we were going to crash so I braced myself hard against the door frame and placed my hand on the release straps of my harness. Looking out at the uneven ground beneath, I knew that when we hit, we would roll over so I would have to escape. At around 20ft above the deck, our co-pilot Marty managed to take control and pulled in power, and we climbed away from the ground.

Not dead ... yet. We gathered our composure and assessed the damage while putting a radio call out to our playmate aircraft who was in the air above us. (We always flew in pairs so that if one aircraft went down the other could in theory pick the crew and passengers up.) The cockpit glass had been shattered, hence the reason our pilot could not see as some had gone into his eyes, but he was fine. All the systems seemed OK, but unlike back in Blighty, we couldn't simply 'land on' to carry out a full assessment, as we were in a war zone. Our playmate came in close to fly by our side and try and assess the damage from their aircraft. We limped back to Bastion at low level in case we had to land immediately at any point. This was THE longest forty-five minutes of my life. I moved my weapon and 'go' bag full of bullets and water right by my side for the whole transit back. We made it to Bastion safely and shut down to be met by our boss, OC 1310 Flight. He was just glad to see we were all OK, sadly the aircraft was not and was parked up in the hangar for some major repairs. Now what was funny about all of this is that at the time of the accident England were playing in the World Cup. The set of pylons that we hit supplied all the electricity down the Helmand Valley, and we pulled the plug out effectively right in the middle of the game. Doh, sorry lads. I phoned Skelfy that night from the little phone booths on camp. He said it was the first time he had heard me cry. The next day my brother popped over to our tent. He was deployed at Bastion at the same time as me as an engineer with the Army Lynx Helicopter Detachment. His opening line, 'Have you seen that Chinook parked up in the hangar, Liz? Who were the crew on that? They are lucky to be alive.'

'Er yeah, on that note Graham, don't tell Mum.'

Chapter 8

Gloria

I next deployed to Op Herrick in December that same year. The Chinook fleet at the time had both 18 and 27 Squadron covering this deployment, both with an A and B Flight of twenty aircrew each, which equated to five crews. This basically meant as a Flight we deployed together every eight months or so, doing a two-month stint as that was the maximum we could do before having to return for various flying currencies in the UK. This roulement lead to me deploying on Op Herrick ten times in total from 2006 until 2014. I was not unique in reaching double figures as a small handful of my colleagues also amassed a dismaying amount of time away. We used to joke that we should buy property out there as we visited so often, and it really did start to feel like home in many ways. This Christmas detachment, despite being away from family, was not too bad. Like many things in life, the idea of it was worse than the reality and once we were out in theatre, we just mentally disengaged from what we were missing and got on with the task at hand. Skelfy had engineered to deploy to Kandahar for the same months that I would be there, so we managed to spend some limited time together. The weather was miserable out in Afghanistan in the winter months though, so it was lots of sitting on the sofas in the coffee shops and nowhere near as much fun as Basra in the sunshine. Skelfy had given me a huge green coat that was only issued to the SF sniper soldiers – in thickness it resembled five sleeping bags stitched together. He also had one and there was much banter to be had as we walked around in matching his and hers coats. But those that mocked secretly wanted one as the Afghan winter is hideously cold, and we spent most of our days flying at 3,000ft above mean sea level (AMSL) with the doors wide open as we had the guns fitted and therefore couldn't pull down the upper hatch to seal the cabin from the wind. Anything you could put on to warm up when you landed was always an essential piece of kit and my coat was borrowed many times. The fact that when I wore it, I pretty much trebled my silhouette in size was always hilarious: tiny girl, gigantic coat! The force were also starting to get busy now tasking-wise as Bastion grew in size and the army deployed even more British troops further up the Helmand Valley. The month running up to Christmas was mainly spent ferrying hundreds of bags of mail around the Helmand Valley to all of our troops living out in the remote FOBs. The UK were running a system where anyone could send a welfare parcel out to those deployed and it would be given to a soldier out in Helmand somewhere. That year we routinely filled the aircraft cabin up to bursting point, covering up the windows with strops so that no stray bags could fall out as we stacked them up past the level of the windows. We were like Santa's sleigh and each time the ramp went down I loved seeing the smiles on the faces of our troops as we handed them bags and bags of letters and parcels from home, forming a little chain of merry men at the ramp as they offloaded them into their wagon. One of the places we were tasked to fly was an American base up in Tarin Kowt about an hour north of Kandahar. This will go down as one of the most surreal dinners of my life. We shut down and went in search of the food hall before heading to a brief about an Op we were due to do with the Yanks. At the door was an enormous 7ft inflatable turkey and we dined on pumpkin pie and all things Thanksgiving with some totally confused Afghan soldiers. We also had a big 'exfil' task on Christmas Eve ('exfil' is a term we use when we recover troops out of the battlefield), to pull a lot of the 'SF' lads back into the main base in time for Christmas Day. Three aircraft spent the day filling up with troops, kit, vehicles, as much as we could fit in each time and flying them back to KAF. On this task my squadron boss continued to land and get us to jam more in until they were almost sitting on top of one another with kit rammed under the seats. We managed to get the job done earlier than expected and the lads were so chuffed to get back to a hot shower and food early that they invited us up for beers in their bar. Now, unlike Iraq, Afghanistan was a completely 'dry' deployment for us as we had to be fit to crew in at any time due to the threat level. That meant no drinking and there were no bars around camp, except of course for the SF bar, as they make their own rules (ha-ha).

So, we ran it past the boss, and he said a few of us could go up for one or two beers. Skelfy came and collected us and off we went. It was so cold in this outside shed bar that we were all standing around in big coats with tins of Stella or Strongbow in our pockets. The rest of the crewmen headed off and I stayed on to sneak a night stay up at Skelfy's tent. We managed to snuggle to keep warm on the tiny cot bed and it was nice to be able to fall asleep with him. However, I woke up the next morning, Christmas Day, to see one of Skelfy's flip flops float past my face. The tent had flooded overnight, in fact the whole camp area had; it resembled the Somme when we went out to have a look. Luckily, that day I was programmed as duty driver for the crews rather than flying. So I spent Christmas Day 2006 driving around a swamp in a Land Rover covered in mud, with a hangover. The only thing that made the day 'Merry' was that the Royal Marines decided to do a section run around camp wearing nothing but Santa hats. I may have got stuck behind them in my Land Rover ... I didn't try to overtake, far too risky, yep, definitely just stick where I am.

By the time my next deployment came in 2007 I had been posted to 18 Squadron. It was common to do around three years as a posting and then, if you requested, move on for a fresh start. I wanted to become a Crewman Trainer and 18 Squadron offered me this career progression, so I took it. The Chinook Detachment (which was collectively referred to as 1310 Flt) also had now started to fly 50/50 from Camp Bastion as well as Kandahar. Our accommodation at Bastion was a basic 12ft x12ft army tent rather than the American hardened accommodation blocks back at KAF. It was pretty basic, but we made it home with the addition of some Ikea furniture and we always took our own duvet covers with us for our little cot beds. I had a pink combat one. I was always allowed to have the bed in the corner so I could hang up a flag and a towel to give myself a little shelter to get changed in. I became an expert in that dance we all do when trying to get changed at the beach without everyone seeing! But I would not have wanted to be anywhere else, despite the offerings of a female tent. That would have been isolating and lonely, I wanted to be with the lads who were also my best mates. Eventually, after a few years we moved into metal buildings called Tier 2 at Bastion rather than tents and we had separate rooms to share with crewmates. My most fun 'roomie' of course was Grohly when I volunteered to go out on a deployment with B Flight from 18 Squadron to work for my other great friend, Ginge, who was the crewman leader at the time. I arrived halfway through the detachment to be met by them both at the airhead in Bastion and they took me up to the accommodation and showed me to the little room that Grohly and I would be sharing as we were crewed up together. They had turned the end of the room into a little pink palace for me with a princess duvet cover and a pink curtain to draw across, so I had some privacy to get changed etc.!

Everything was ramping up now threat-wise in Helmand. I used to refer to this as my 'normality' bar. When I first arrived in Basra aged 21, and we were tasked to go land at Basra Palace for example, it had been rocketed or mortared the week before. I remember thinking, oh blimey that's exciting but dangerous. I have written that sentence deliberately in that order, as honestly, danger was always the afterthought for us. We were tasked to go somewhere so we went, we did not question it. Next time I would be on an aircraft landing at a site that had been rocketed the day before. Then next time it had been mortared that morning before we were due in. Slowly with exposure to these occurrences my tolerance for what was dangerous went up. Rather hilariously our crew were tasked into a landing site at Now Zad for the very purpose of being mortared. This sounded as ludicrous to us as it probably does to you! The landing site was constantly being rocketed, but British troops on the ground couldn't identify the Taliban firing point. Op 'Tethered Goat' was dreamt up so we could go and land – obviously a massive bloody target – then wait until we got fired upon therefore allowing our guys to locate the Taliban's position. Basically, we were a huge piece of cheese in a mouse trap. Thankfully, someone somewhere saw sense, and this crazy idea was pulled by the heads of sheds. Being cleared into land when there was a break in the incoming fire was, however, becoming 'normal' and wouldn't faze us. Eventually, landing under fire didn't even fluster us as much as you would expect, especially when we had to rescue casualties. Of course, we had 'actions on' when we came under 'contact', i.e. enemy fire, but this usually came with the caveat that we would only lift when safe to do so, i.e. all troops safely on or off the aircraft. I still remember the first time we were sitting on a landing site when we came under 'contact'. The aircraft rotor noise is so loud that at first you don't hear it. The first thing you notice is the dust being kicked up off the ground surrounding the aircraft as the bullets get closer, then the distinctive 'ting, ting, ting' as they begin to hit the metal of the aircraft frame. Because it's so hard to identify a firing point where the rounds are coming from, you just have to stand your ground at the minigun and pray that there's a little 'Ready Brek' glow surrounding you, making you bulletproof. This little halo has indeed saved me twice. The first time was a bullet going into the aircraft less than a foot above my head. We were on a landing site loading troops and heard the distinctive and sporadic hollow 'ting' noise as rounds came through the aircraft skin. We got the last troop safely over the ramp and lifted immediately. On returning to Bastion, the engineers did the battle damage assessment to discover we had been pepper-potted with a few small arms rounds, one of which had left a bullet hole large enough to get my finger through. The second time was when our ballistic protection panels, which we have fitted to the floor, caught one right under my feet, and without question, saved my life. During an infill for another Deliberate Night Op, out of nowhere I felt a thud through my feet as if the aircraft had been hit by a sledgehammer. We were quite high, and above what we called the 'threat band' where normal calibre bullets of 7.62 would generally run out of momentum. We also took some rounds down around the ramp area and the engines, and it was assessed on landing these where high-calibre anti-aircraft ammunitions (AAA) rounds, hence why they made it as high as our flight level at 3,000ft. The engineers very kindly found the bullets from both of these incidents and gave them to me. They live in my bedside drawer, maybe I should make a set of earrings out of them. People used to say 'you are so brave', but the reality is being shot at is like crossing the road and nearly getting hit by a car. By the time it's happened you are past the point of danger for the majority of 'contacts'. I must admit though, the first time I ever got shot at and could see the Taliban holding the weapon pointing at me, my initial thought was not fear, it was 'cheeky bugger, how dare you' as I manoeuvred my weapon sight on to him.

We all became so immune to the threats we were facing we began to nickname some of the Ops we went on as 'Op Certain Death' much to our boss's dismay. The first of these big Op Certain Deaths was in 2007 when we were part of the massive Heli Assault mission to take Musa Quala from Taliban control. This was a combined Operation with both us and the Yanks, with the odd Dutch Chinook added in for good measure, along with Apaches and various other flying elements providing top cover. The lead-up to this Op went on for days at Kandahar and involved a mass briefing for all the aircrew and various 'walk-through rock drills in the hangar'. When we came out of the final briefing we had a team photo, which once again added to the immensity of the impending doom as we had NEVER done this before. I could almost envision this picture appearing in a museum next to a Battle of Britain picture commemorating 'the few' in the Taking of Musa Quala. What didn't help matters was that while we had all been inside briefing, the American padre (priest) had been around all the aircraft with his 'Holy Oil' and had blessed all the weapons fitted to our aircraft – which we discovered during our walk rounds. There were sixteen aircraft in total in our assault package and thankfully we had the British padre on board with us, some small reassurance that we may be shielded from bullets by his halo in the jump seat. The only thing that having the padre on board did in fact provide, though, was an outbreak of Tourette's amongst the crew. It's a common affliction that anytime you are within earshot of a padre you can't help yourself but swear more, despite best efforts. Due to the fact that you are reading about this Op in my book and not in countless historical books about the helicopter carnage of Musa Quala you may have guessed that it went off without much in way of incidents. In the main, 'Op Certain Death' was actually 'Op Damp Squid' for the air package anyhow, but Musa Quala was taken, so 'mission accomplished', home for tea and medals. Many, many, more 'Op Certain Deaths' were flown by many other crews including myself over the years, most of which went without incident, as the Taliban weren't stupid and had usually poked off by the time we got there with our three Chinooks and 120 troops. It was the days that you weren't expecting it that usually caught you out the most, as I mentioned earlier.

The Chinook is a mighty beast though, which I will come to later. It can take a lot of battle damage yet still remain airborne and can lift much more in reality than the figures in any performance graph would have you believe. Before flying, we would always brief these important figures such as maximum performance and safe single engine weight, i.e. the weight at which if we lost an engine we could stay airborne. I have never in all my time on the fleet had to unload freight as we simply could not lift, quite the opposite in fact. One of my favourite moments regarding this was the Christmas Eve 'exfil', mentioned earlier, with OC 27 Squadron Wing Commander Shell (or Shelly as he was known). We were 'exfiling' the SBS (Special

Boat Service) from an Op they had conducted in the Panjsway Valley. I always found it ironic that we had the SBS operating in Afghanistan when there wasn't a boat in sight. As we lifted, Shelly the boss realised he had loads more power so he landed on. We filled up with more troops and kit then re-lifted to the hover. Once again, he set the aircraft back down and repeated 'more'. We ended up with troops and kit stashed everywhere, all the way to the roof, but we took off with power in hand. We also used to 'bend' the rules somewhat when it came to getting guys out of the FOBs who were headed home for R and R (Rest and Recuperation). This was a two-week window the ground troops were given during their tour to get home and see their loved ones. The big flaw in this procedure, however, was that their two-week clock started ticking before they had left theatre, therefore every minute they spent waiting for flights meant less time back with their loved ones. It would be catastrophic if they missed the TriStar they were booked on to fly home to the UK as the next one could be as far off as six days later, so we always did our best to get them back to Bastion. We declared twenty-four seats on our daily tasking line. This meant that the tasking cell who created the manifests would ensure that no matter who got on or off at each location we would only ever have twenty-four passengers on board at any given time, so maybe six off, four on, next site two off, four on and we as crewmen managed this along with the Jenga puzzle of people's kit at each location. However, sometimes, in fact most of the time, the tasking sheet NEVER reflected what came towards the ramp when we lowered it. Many times we were greeted with more freight and passengers than expected and much swearing and hand gesturing began. There was, however, no chance of me turning away a soldier heading home on R and R because we were 'full'. I would always find space even if that meant giving up my crash seat at the rear. This was just another troop seat, not specifically designed or labelled in any way as 'reserved for crew' so it was common to load troops and turn around to see one of them grinning at you from your seat with a thumbs up as he secured himself with his lap strap. Technically it was frowned upon to give up your crash seat but nearly all crewmen did as we walked around the cabin on our harness most of the time and truth be told if we were going to crash most of us would want to be laid flat on the floor or next to the nearest big exit, i.e., the ramp. Talking of crash positions, it is a well-known fact that the step ladder always survives any aircraft crash. Sadly, a few of my mates have attended crash sites shortly after the accident and the one thing that always stands out intact amongst the wreckage is the ladder. So, if I'm honest, strapping yourself to the step ladder prior to 'piling' in was probably the safest bet for survival! During the really overburdened days all it took was a nod to the other crewman at the front to pull across the dust curtain between the cabin and the cockpit as we loaded up. This curtain was pulled across on approach to land to prevent dust getting into the cockpit. But the upshot was it trapped the heat in the cockpit and the pilots always asked if we could pull it open while loading the cabin. The dust curtain was the bane of most crewmen's lives. It had a strip of Velcro along its sides that was meant to fasten to the Velcro on the metal frame each side of the cockpit entrance. The more dust that got engrained in the Velcro the less effective it became and barely ever stayed put. The result being that most of the time on landing it would get sucked into the cockpit with a flurry of powder-like dust anyhow. But when we did pull it across on the ground the cockpit couldn't see in the mirror the chaos being stacked up in the cabin, then when they asked prior to lifting 'what POB?' we were, the answer was always twenty-four pax, four crew. They must have been laughing their asses off as they pulled in twice as much power as would be needed for twenty-eight people on board. But for the purposes of the intercom and therefore the flight deck recorder we were all above board. That's what the Chinook force did. We supported our troops on the ground and we got the job done, even if it was a little 'untidy' at times. And they were 'our' troops. I felt it was my personal responsibility to look after each and every one of them into and out of the battlefield in whatever form that took. As the years went by, I couldn't tell if I was just getting older or the troops were getting younger but by my last few Op Herricks I was carrying in the cabin what felt like kids, almost too young to be allowed out after dark, never mind run out of the ramp of a Chinook into battle.

It was an aircrew thing to have a spare name badge with something amusingly cryptic written on it such as Hugh Jarse or Imac Hunt. Sometime along the years Skelfy nicknamed me 'Gloria Stitz'. I had a helmet badge made up in black with 'Gloria Stitz' written on it in pink, rather than our usual green and black badges. I enjoyed watching it make some of the troops laugh as they spotted it, providing they got the joke. I wore it for all my Op Herrick deployments, and it almost became my alias, while I was at war.

When holding MERT standby, we left our flying kit prepped and ready on the aircraft for the full twenty-four hours of standby so we could crew in as fast as possible when the call came. Each morning and evening we would go out to the aircraft to carry out a kit check and a walk around. One morning I walked out and noticed my Gloria badge had gone from the back of my helmet. I was gutted and was sure it had been nicked by someone, as people used to wander over to our aircraft to get photos standing next to the minigun all the time. A few days later, we were back on the normal tasking line and were off to recover some troops that we had dropped into the Sangin Valley the previous week. As these guys were coming up the ramp, one stopped and pointed at me then began to pat his trouser pockets down. He pulled out my Gloria badge and shouted in my ear as best he could, 'I found this attached to my Bergen last week.' My badge must have been ripped off as these guys had been running past me during the infill, which could easily be done. The chances of me picking up the same guy on my aircraft a week later were slim to none! I was so chuffed to have my beloved badge back, covered in Helmand dust. Gloria had been into the battlefield and made it out alive!

One of my more memorable trips involving 'Gloria' on Op Herrick was taking Ross Kemp into Musa Qala, which was now under British Forces control, for his documentary. We took off that day with an aircraft full of troops along with Ross Kemp and his film crew. He was seated opposite me on the aircraft just next to the ramp. My other crewman up front dared me to write to him on one of our sick bags, which was our very basic method of communicating with our passengers over the noise. The message was, 'Which one of these TWATS is Ross Kemp then?' Smiling I got a sick bag down from behind my head and in big letters jotted the note, before holding it up to show around to all the passengers including him, he laughed and raised his middle finger in jest. Then he reached over his head and pulled another sick bag down and started writing. When he held it up it read: 'Which one of these TWATS is your boyfriend then?' It made me blush and laugh out loud. Soon enough I was manning the M60 on the ramp as we made our approach to land at Musa Qala, which was still a fairly dangerous site. The second our wheels touched on it was ramp down, all hands-on-deck to unload the cabin before the inevitable incoming fire began. Ross Kemp worked like a demon helping to get kit off, not just his stuff, but all the soldiers' Bergens as well. I had a newfound respect for him, as unlike other journalists, and celebrities I'd flown before he wasn't shy of getting stuck in when needed. We collected him a few days later and recovered him back to Kandahar. That evening he was doing a 'meet and greet' at the NAAFI coffee shop on base. My other crewmate Toddy went along and was chatting away to him about his visit. He said that a female crewman had taken him into Musa Qala, called Gloria Stitz? It took Toddy a few seconds then he piped up, 'Oh you mean Liz.' Kemp replied, 'nope this girl was definitely called Gloria.' To which Toddy said, 'Yep but her real name is Liz.' Ross still did not get it. A year later, one of our pilots John was attending the Sun Military or 'Milly' awards to receive the Airman of the Year prize. This was an awards dinner set up for forces but full of celebrities and he was sitting at a table next to Kemp. They got chatting over dinner and Ross brought up the fact that a crewman called Gloria Stitz had taken him into Musa Qala on a Chinook. It took John a little longer to figure out who he was on about but then replied 'Ah, you mean Liz?' … to which Kemp replied, 'Yeah someone else said that, must be a different girl.' Priceless. I recently watched him on ITV while he was helping out with the Poppy Appeal in London for the Armed Forces Poppy Day. No matter what anyone says, Ross Kemp has single-handedly shone a light on the missions and the struggles that the British Forces encounter. Before Kemp, very few of the general public had an insight into the front line, and what being a soldier in a conflict zone is like. He also continues to support many of the Veteran community and is constantly raising awareness on issues like PTSD. I have a huge amount of respect for him after flying him that day and he's absolutely changed my mind about war journalism over the years with his supportive and informative stance. Still makes me giggle though every time I see him on TV!

Chapter 9

The Greatest Honour

I often refer to my time in Helmand as 'the best of times and the worst of times'. As I mentioned earlier, one of our roles in Afghanistan was to hold the IRT (Immediate Response Team) with a crew always on standby at fifteen minutes notice to move by day and thirty minutes notice to move by night, so we could sleep. I will state right now, for the record, that these were limits not targets. I don't think it ever took a crew longer than ten minutes to get airborne, even from the deepest sleep, the norm was around five minutes. This was because the IRT aircraft was the flying ambulance that recovered our wounded soldiers from the battlefield, and we treated this task with the greatest respect. We had a team of four medics and six force protection soldiers that held the duty with us. Over the years it was renamed to MERT which stands for 'Medical Emergency Response Team' which was created purely for Operation Herrick, and we were given the callsign 'Tricky 73'. This callsign became renowned around theatre and when you heard 'Tricky 73' bell up on frequency, all the other aircraft would minimise comms to allow this callsign free airwaves to talk to HQ or ground callsigns. In the early days, each crew held the duty for a week at a time living in our tent beside the Ops room at Bastion, with an aircraft full of med kit, strapped and stowed wherever we could fit it. By 2007, the war had become much more kinetic, with soldiers being killed or injured now an almost daily occurrence. It became the norm to arrive back at the flight line to shut down and hand the aircraft back to our engineers who would wash the blood off the floor in the cabin. Looking back now that must have taken its toll on so many of them as they could do nothing yet sweep up the aftermath but hadn't directly been able to be part of the rescue mission. What they did in terms of getting and keeping that aircraft ready to fly was outstanding and the MERT couldn't have done its job without them doing theirs so professionally in the background. The MERT aircraft was soon fitted out with a full rubber mat floor and the MOST amazing medical kit, all with its exact place so it could be located instantly in the dark, while trying to save lives. The bosses eventually decided to reduce the duty to twenty-four hours at a time as it had become so traumatic, with days of relentless high-octane flying and *M.A.S.H*-like scenes in the cabin. They were worried about the mental toll it was taking on the crews. Sadly, by the time this change came into effect a lot of the irreparable damage had been done and would go on to haunt them forever.

The way the MERT worked was as follows: when a soldier was injured out in the field, his colleagues would get on the radio to Battle HQ with what was called a '9-liner'. A 9-liner was a clearly laid out list that all soldiers used to pass the details of the incident, consisting of location, callsign, number and type of injuries, enemy threat etc. … It was so important that we all used this format as inevitably adrenaline was high when these messages were being passed. Even if the radio had interference or another transmission came over the top you would be able to gather the main details, as your brain was expecting them to come in this precise order. The casualties were labelled as A, B and C – or T1, 2, 3 or T4 when we moved to the American system – to denote the extent of their injuries. T1 was the worst casualty with severe life-threatening injuries, T2 would be slightly more stable, T3 walking wounded and T4 was deceased or KIA. These 9-liners would sometimes come to us over the radio while we were already airborne or via Bastion Ops if we were sitting in the tent. We had a green field phone hanging in the corner of our tent. It was very basic, so it had the same ringtone for all calls around the network. The way the system was set up though, is that if it rang once it was an IRT shout and if a second ring followed it was an admin call about niff naff and trivia. When this phone rang, adrenaline spiked and we all stopped and waited for the second ring; if this happened it was back to watching TV. If it DIDN'T ring a second time it was all systems go. In hindsight this was a crap system as throughout the day your adrenaline would surge unnecessarily, which in itself caused many PTSD-related issues further down the line. If it was a 9-liner call everyone would scream 'shout' at the top of our lungs and the engineers would ring a large bell. This was done so we could alert as many people around us as to what was happening. The medics would get the same call next door, as did the force protection from their tent and you could hear the dreaded single ring rippling along the two tents after we had the first alert.

What happened next was a sea of people sprinting towards the aircraft in various states of dress, sometimes while throwing on their combat shirts or T-shirts having been sitting in the sun. The engineers would help get us ready to lift and would be crawling all over the aircraft removing covers and ropes as required; the medics would be prepping their equipment and the force protection guys would be putting on their headsets and body armour. It was well co-ordinated chaos, but everyone knew exactly what they should be doing, resulting in the slickest aircraft start every time. While all this was happening, one of the crewmen would stay back by the phone that had originally rung and take the 9-liner details before catching the crew up mid-start; meanwhile, the other crewman had begun racing through the checks solo with both the pilots. This is why everyone had to be top of their game, as quite often you found yourself having to now cover two lots of checks or putting the grid into the navigation kit while the pilots armed up the aircraft and started the engines with you listening in. On top of all this, everyone was moving at warp speed, doing lots of their individual tasks and checks concurrently.

The process to getting the MERT aircraft airborne was incredibly well-polished, so much so, even I was in awe as to just how quickly we could lift. One minute watching *Game of Thrones*, four minutes later departing Bastion, and loading the weapons. Sometimes going from being fast asleep to flying into a dark, dusty landing site in a hail of bullets fifteen minutes later, with your pyjamas still on under your flying kit. Not all heroes wear capes!

On landing at the location of the casualty, the ramp would go down and the force protection team would run off to surround the aircraft with fire positions while the combat medics made their way to the casualty. The combat medics were amazing, and I was always in awe as they ran off into the unknown without hesitation to meet the troops carrying or dragging the broken body. The stretcher or walking wounded would then be carried up over the ramp. We would always put the toe ramps out as trying to step up on to the aircraft when carrying a fully laden soldier on a stretcher was a challenge for even the strongest of men. Next, the force protection collapsed back in (when it was safe to do so) and threw themselves into their seats. Finally, we would do a quick head count. Firstly, to make sure we had all our medics and protection guys back on; secondly, to ensure we had all the casualties we expected now safely loaded on to the aircraft. This was trickier than it sounds as there were medics now on the floor crouched around stretchers, soldiers bringing weapons and kit belonging to the wounded soldier aboard and the odd time a new walking wounded whom we may not have expected. Finally, once sure we had everyone and having given a new folded-up stretcher to the intact troops as they ran back off the ramp, we would lift for the fastest route back to Bastion regardless of ground threat. Once airborne, we would ask the doctor on headset if they wanted us to fly as quickly as possible, but this could mean a bumpier ride, or high and smooth depending on the nature of the injuries. As we raced back to Bastion, the No. 2 crewman would be on the radio to Ops to let them know any updates on the casualty's condition and an ETA so they could relay to the hospital and the doctors could prepare for what was coming. If blood was required, which happened a lot, we would pass the call 'Op Vampire'. We would then land on at 'Nightingale' the helicopter landing site right next to Bastion hospital and be met by the appropriate number of ambulances and the fire crews who always helped the medics offload the casualties. Once loaded, the ambulances would make the short 20-metre journey to the hospital entrance where the injured would be put back together again by the most amazing medical staff in the British military. Bastion was the most advanced field hospital in the world at that time. At one point, it was said you had more chance of surviving a non-survivable injury in Afghanistan than anywhere else on the planet.

Nightingale HLS was not far from the cook house, so if you were walking to and from the food hall you would see the aircraft come into land and your heart would sink. If the casualty had serious injuries or had died then you would hear the words 'Op Minimise, Op Minimise, Op Minimise' echo around the entire camp via the monotone and soulless tannoy system. Op Minimise meant that all the external communications on camp were disconnected so you couldn't call home or use the internet. This was put in place to ensure that the family of those involved in a catastrophic incident got the news first via the correct channels and not through the 'jungle drums' of squaddies on camp. Sometimes it only lasted a few hours, and sometimes it was in place for days. With each minute that it dragged on I always felt sick in my stomach knowing that the family had not yet been informed what had happened and had no idea that their son had died or been critically maimed in action. I always wondered whether a mother could feel it in her heart the second her son's had stopped beating and if by some sixth sense they knew. I use the term son generically as I only ever collected male soldiers, but I know that we have females who also have paid the ultimate price in conflict. When people whinged about no internet due to Minimise, I would get very angry, very quickly. I'm one of the calmest people you could ever meet but this instantly riled me. My answer between gritted teeth was 'Count yourself lucky that in a few days YOU can call your loved ones and tell them you're OK and they aren't receiving a call at the front door from the Officer Commanding in his best uniform.' The only other thing that used to 'light my blue touch paper' was people who asked if they could go to the gym rather than the sunset ramp ceremonies to honour the fallen as they were flown out of Camp Bastion at the start of their repatriation journey. These were mandatory for all personnel not on duty, but even that devalued them in my opinion. I believe every single person on that camp should have wanted, in fact been honoured, to attend this ceremony. Watching the coffins of our fallen heroes who had paid the ultimate price being carried on to the waiting Hercules draped in a Union Jack never failed to bring me to silent rolling tears. The Last Post followed by the engines of the Hercules being spun up did little to muffle the sound of sniffling tears throughout the rank and file, followed by pure silence as the aircraft flew off into their last Afghan sunset for their final journey home.

All the above I have described using the term casualty as in singular, but more often than not it was multiple casualties. The 9-liners could be two T1s, three T2s and one T3 or a mix of all. When you heard this, you knew the scene was going to be carnage when you arrived and sometimes en route to the pick-up point we would fold up all the seats against the wall to fit as many stretchers in as possible. We could fit seven stretchers in with all the extra medic kit stacked around the walls. When I say some days resembled a scene from the TV series *M.A.S.H* I am not exaggerating. A casualty at war has usually resulted from an incident with the enemy. This could be a gun fight or an IED that had blown their vehicle or their bodies to pieces. And it was usual to see stretchers coming over the ramp reflecting these mechanisms of injury, from heads shot open to legs and arms missing. I will not cover any specific details as they will still be so raw for many soldiers, families, colleagues, and friends involved. Watching the medics at work saving lives and limbs down the back of our aircraft is something that I will remain in awe of forever. They were absolutely the best in their field and unflappable. They would run off the ramp into the battlefield to collect casualties, they would put cannulas into arms while being thrown around as we evaded bullets and they would bring back those who were on the brink of death right in front of my eyes. All of this sometimes done in the dark while holding a torch in their mouth as for tactical reasons we couldn't put the cabin lights on. The Op Herrick MERT medics were flying angels.

There are a few days that stick in my mind though. One of which was my busiest day on MERT (or IRT at the time as this was in 2008). On that particular day, we amassed a total of fourteen shouts. It was relentless. We landed at Nightingale and offloaded one casualty just as another 9-liner was coming through on the radio. At one point we were being informed of incoming 9-liners while still ten minutes flying away from Bastion with a cabin already full of injured bodies. There were troops in contact all day and I have never known anything like it. There was also one job where five British soldiers had been killed in one incident up at FOB Whishtun. We flew in and landed on to collect our fallen soldiers. Each stretcher had a flag over the body, I remember the Union Jack, the Rifles flag, and a Liverpool flag. Still to this day I really struggle to see a Union Jack flag without getting overwhelmed with memories, and Remembrance Day I find harder each year. The thing that stayed with me most though was this: the love our British soldiers have for their brothers in arms. Watching them carry their best mates who had paid the ultimate price over our ramp while trying to hold their emotions together was the hardest sight of it all, despite all the blood and gore. Knowing that in that instant there are no words or smiles you can give them that will take that pain away, and you know, as well as they do, that they must go back into the fight and carry on regardless. Once I watched as our medics fought to save a young soldier's life at my feet. His mate had been injured too but was T3 and sitting on the seat next to me. You know the moment that the soul has slipped away from a body, as the medics heads initially fall, then they look up at one another. I knew he had gone, and so did his friend who was watching on. In that moment all I wanted to do was hug him and tell him it was OK to cry as I saw his eyes glaze. But he did not, and I wondered if he had no emotions left after what they had been through. Making the radio call back to Ops to update them that a T1 was now a T4 was the worst part of my job and was always done with a lump in my throat.

Another memory that has stayed with me was collecting a Royal Marine who had been killed by enemy fire up at Kajaki Dam. When we landed, his mates carried his body on in a sealed-up body bag. It had a piece of tape across the bag with his rank and name on it. We flew him home to Bastion from where his repatriation journey home to the UK continued. We used to try our best not to make a habit of visiting casualties we had brought back to the hospital. Maybe the odd one or two who we knew had made it, but otherwise it became too personal. It was easier to compartmentalise if you just envisioned that you were carrying a precious piece of kit. So, a year or two later I was back in the UK and out with Skelfy reading the Sunday papers over a coffee. I suddenly burst into tears and Skelfy turned to ask what was wrong. I had just read the story of this soldier in the *Sunday Times*. He had proposed to his girlfriend before he had deployed and there were pictures of them as a couple and him in uniform. It hit me like a tonne of bricks as there was now a story and a face behind that body bag.

There were, of course, some other unique moments on MERT that didn't have quite such an intense consequence. One that springs to mind was when we were called to go and recover an ANA soldier (Afghan National Army) with a gunshot wound to both legs and his hand. This was all the information we had as we set off swiftly to recover him back to Bastion. It turns out that this soldier had decided he no longer wished to serve with the ANA and the best course of action to leave was to shoot himself in the hand and be discharged. Well on attempting to carry out his ridiculous plan he couldn't stop his hand from shaking so he steadied it on his leg. He ended up shooting HIMSELF through his hand, into his knee and the bullet then ricocheted into his other knee cap. Another, rather amusing, moment was when we got tasked up to Kajaki to recover a Parachute Regiment soldier who had jumped off the top of the 40ft water tower at the dam as a bet and on hitting the water had 'split his "ass" open' (to quote the doctor). Thankfully, both of these chaps survived their self-inflicted injuries but there is something to be said for the Darwin theory, had they not.

We didn't just recover British soldiers from the battlefield but also any other national troops who needed us. I have, during my time on MERT, been tasked to collect an injured Taliban soldier which brought a whole different turmoil of emotions as I watched him being loaded on to the aircraft alongside our British soldiers who had been injured by his actions – his intent to kill them.

The last body I picked up during my time in Helmand was an American soldier who had been killed near FOB Edinburgh, halfway up the Helmand Valley. The US refer to their fallen soldiers as 'angels' which always makes my spine tingle when I hear it over the radio net. We landed on and shut down as the stretcher draped in the Stars and Stripes made its way towards our ramp. When his body had been loaded on, one of the team of US medics handed me his foot in a separate clear bag. It tells me a lot about how my own mental state was by this time of the campaign as even this didn't make me bat an eyelid or flinch. I had become the master of blocking out emotions to get the task done and almost immune to feeling sorrow. On return to Bastion, I headed back up to my room, which I didn't share with anyone and had been locked all day. I walked in to find an American rank slide sitting square in the middle of the floor, next to my bunk bed. They say white feathers are a sign of loved ones sending a sign and I often wonder if this little badge was a similar sign from that angel as there was no other explanation for it being there. But the greatest sum of casualties by far were the men, women and children of Afghanistan who got caught in the crossfire while others fought over their country

Crewing the MERT aircraft was an honour. It was a privilege to be part of our soldiers' final journey and it will remain with me forever as the greatest purpose of my career. However, I often look back now since we have pulled our troops out of Helmand and wonder if it was worth it for the lives lost. I have discussed it with many Herrick Veterans. Nearly all say that being at war was in truth the one time they felt alive, which I completely resonate with. They joined to do a job, and yes some fell, but they died doing the job they loved. I can take some comfort in this. After a heavy day on MERT I used to get a coffee and go and lie outside on the concrete blast wall beside the tent. In the summer it was always warm and comforting on my back, so I almost melted away in my thoughts while processing the day's events. The Afghan desert has a unique smell to it by day and by night. You can almost tell when the sun has slipped away even when your eyes are closed as the aroma changes. And then the 'call to prayer' breaks the silence. This is the ritual prayers that the Islamic faith sing out loud as the sun goes down. I do not understand a word of what they are calling out, nor really the intent, but the melody of this prayer became strangely familiar and relaxing in this far away land. As I lay there, I always said my own little prayer for the girlfriends, fiancées, and sisters of each fallen warrior, as that's the position I was always most scared to be in. Their world was about to be shattered and their hero was about to become just a heartbroken memory.

For each of our fallen, at the going down of the sun and in the morning, I will always remember you.

The colours of their brothers

Our world is decorated, but obliviously we walk past,
And mostly only notice, when they are brought to half-mast.

In the country I grew up in, there was one for each side,
A flag can unite us, but just as easily divide.

And then after I joined up, they suddenly meant more,
Each time that I saw one, my tears would now pour.

The red, white, and blue, that bled into that cotton,
Watching six of our men carry him, draped in a coffin.

Then the bloodiest day, for our own British troops,
When all in one sitting, we lost five sets of boots.

A mix of football and regiment flags, as the stretchers went past,
Each soldier tucked under, asleep ever last.

Yes, each flag was different, but all the same side,
United by the country, they fought for and died.

I imagine that triangle, handed over with sorrow,
To the family of each soldier, who gave his tomorrow.

And I watch from the ramp, as they stand and dwell,
Then touch for the last time, their brothers who fell.

GS

Chapter 10

The Times in Between

Now it has to be said, although I did spend a LOT of time at war during my years on the Chinook fleet it wasn't always bullets and body armour. We actually went to some nice places too. Mostly in search of dust though as that is the one thing 'we all loved or B ...' a term we used a lot to mean we hated it, but sadly dust training and learning how to safely land in it, is an essential part of our work-up training before deploying. I'd like to think of myself as a connoisseur of dust these days. Iraq had coarse dust that took much longer to pick up with our airflow and fell from the sky quickly once dislodged by our downwash. Afghan dust, however, was like talcum powder. Fine and light, therefore much more dangerous to us. As we come into land anywhere, from around 40ft on the approach, our downwash starts to pick things up off the ground. This can be anything from freshly cut grass, portaloos, tents and marquees, small children and even the odd granny. But we have the luxury, most of the time, to avoid these or overshoot if we do indeed start to create a wake of carnage as we come into land. Sadly though, this cannot be said for dust. We need to get on to the ground regardless but must learn to land safely as the lower you get to the ground the more dust you kick up, and the slower you make your approach, the quicker the dust cloud engulfs you. So basically, dust landings are a balancing act of outrunning the thing and the crewman keeping the pilot updated on the height below the aircraft versus the position of the cloud as it catches up with the cockpit. The key is to be '10' or below before it's a complete dust-out for them so they can actually see the ground they are landing on.

May I add this doesn't always happen as planned and many times we as a whole crew have surprised ourselves by walking away from a landing where we all, if being honest, had lost vital references before the wheels hit. There is always a 'get out of jail free' card to be played which is ANYONE on the crew can call 'OVERSHOOT' if they are not happy with how the landing is going. The pilot should always follow this command as the crewman or co-pilot may have seen something he has not that could damage the aircraft – such as a rock, a ditch or even some troops that are formed up below and who would be pretty upset if we landed on their heads. The very odd time, the pilot may call 'references continuing'. Now although this is frowned upon as someone else on board may have seen something, in the worst dust or darkest nights to collect a Cat A casualty I may let them off – providing they are a safe set of hands. Junior pilots don't even try to ignore the crewman when they call an overshoot as the result will most likely be a fire axe in the side of your head from them on landing.

In order to practise this technique, we deployed to various places in search of dust, but where there was less chance of being shot at. The first for me was Morocco. I've already mentioned the highlight of this detachment, which was the Sangho hotel in Marrakech. The first 'decent' hotel I had stayed in, as the helicopter crews, unlike the fixed wing boys and girls from the RAF, were more accustomed to tents on Salisbury Plain. However, the novelty did wear off quickly as we all came down with food poisoning, as I mentioned. I visited Morocco many times as part of my pre-deployment training and always ended up ill. We operated out of a tented camp we called Ram Ram, near Marrakech, but the odd time flew from a place called Ben Guerir which was a relief satellite landing ground an hour's drive north of Marrakech. The journey up there and back daily was tedious, however, mostly lightened by watching the national sport which appeared to be how many things or people can you fit on a moped while trying to overtake a massive coach. I think the best I saw was a husband, wife, son, two chickens and a baby goat. Ben Guerir was basic to say the least. A massive runway and a lonely building that contained the toilets. I always took my chances with the nearest bush as these toilets were not in any way made for females. Now the funny bit of this, however, was that the lads had assumed that the hole in the ground in each cubicle was in fact a 'long drop' type toilet, if you get what I mean, and had therefore been taking care of their slightly more urgent toilet requirements in these cubicles rather than the urinals. Turns out these cubicles where actually showers and the lads had been shitting in them for days before finding out ... the locals must have thought we were a hideous nation of people! On that note, the Moroccan army don't fly very well – like really not well at all. We used to take them up to drop them at various sites to practise their drills and without fail, one soldier was always sick. They would usually manage to find a sick bag, but then the game began. You see, they almost felt ashamed that they had been sick, so would fold up their little bag containing their curried goat in reverse and place it somewhere behind their seat, under their seat, behind a kit bag or anywhere else they could find. This meant that once we eventually shut down for the day and the airflow was no longer refreshing the cabin space, the smell of sick became instantly recognisable. Nearly daily we had to play this awful game of hide and seek the sick bag out there, but at least they used one. The same cannot be said for the Afghan National Army. Whether it was a lack of understanding due to the language barrier, or just pure pride, they refused to use a sick bag if needed. They too were horrendous flyers and would often be sick in the back of the aircraft. The problem was they would find any vessel other than a sick bag to catch it in. This ranged from their pockets to their cupped hands, to the best I saw: a Kevlar helmet. This moment only got worse as I watched the now green-coloured Afghan run off over our ramp, placing his helmet back on his head while the sick oozed over his face. I don't often feel sick on a Chinook but this particular moment I came close.

One of my biggest regrets over the years was not taking more photos of the places I had seen, except the Atlas Mountains. On my first flight up there, in search of some ridges to practise the advanced technique of landing only our aft wheels, one of the crew pointed out Richard Branson's house. I spent the next three weeks constantly snapping his enormous mansion and not much else, as I was so young and had never seen a 'celebrity's' house before. I still look back in my old pink laptop to find folders and folders of his bloody gaff! We also got plenty of chances to head into the souk in Marrakech's medina square. This was a huge market full of spices, foodstuff and local wares. I don't think there's a Chinook crew from that era that didn't come back with either a Fez, a bongo pipe, or a pair of yellow leather 'banana' shoes as we lovingly called them. In the evening, the square would be awash with monkeys, snake charmers, music and food stalls bellowing smoke into the sky. It was an assault on all your senses and you spent most of the first few minutes fighting off the locals trying to take your money in return for a picture of you with their tamed creatures. The souk always reminded me of an Indiana Jones movie. One night a few of us ventured into the main built-up area of the market. This was a labyrinth that you could get lost in for days, quite literally, or disappear in a more sinister fashion. At every turn someone was trying to sell you something. I'm convinced there were hidden tunnels and doors everywhere as it felt as though the same three men would pester you at every fifth stall. It was, however, the sport of the evening to barter with them all and see how low you could get them with their goods, mostly never intending to actually buy anything. At one of these stalls, Streety, one of our pilots, while bartering away jokingly said 'you can have the girl for fifty camels' and pointed at me. Being young and blonde – which was unique for Morocco – as you can imagine, created a whole new bidding game for the evening. This man followed and intercepted us at every turn to add some extra camels to his offer and Streety took great pleasure in stating 'hundred camels or no deal'. As we walked around and the camel offerings climbed, I began to get wearier and wearier as some of his local mates had now come to join in the haggling game. Once we got to eighty camels, Streety eventually gave in and said deal while holding out his hands. The game had become boring now and we were about to head off from the market in search of dinner. I honestly spent the next thirty minutes, as we left the depths of the souk, convinced I was going to be snatched away through some secret door or wall of scarves, never to be seen again. But thankfully the ring of steel, known as the crewmen, bodyguarded me the whole way out … I still didn't relax at dinner that night though.

My favourite memory of my time in Morocco was a good friend DC's last day flying with the Chinook fleet before he left the RAF. That morning I had gone for a run around the edge of the Sango hotel and collected fresh limes. I also filled up a few empty water bottles with fresh orange juice from the breakfast buffet and took my little hip flask filled with Southern Comfort with me and popped it all into my 'go bag' that I would always take flying. Off we set as a crew with DC at the controls and myself and Fryster down the back. We landed on a plateau at 10,000ft which was the maximum height we could fly to. Mainly, as the air is so thin, we were in danger of becoming 'hypoxic' if we spent too long at this altitude. Hypoxia is where your brain slowly becomes starved of oxygen and we train for this in a controlled chamber at RAF Henlow to experience the sensation so you can recognise it in yourself if you do start to become hypoxic, as everyone experiences different symptoms. For me, it felt as though I was drunk when my brain became starved of oxygen, others simply froze, some giggled uncontrollably. On landing at this plateau, I jumped out with the cooler box we had on board for water with a mission to go and gather snow to fill the box. I ran around like a little elf, gathering as much snow as I could into the red box. And throwing snowballs at the cockpit. After a few minutes, Fryster gestured to me to get back on board as I'd clearly lost all track of time and had been running around like a 5-year-old in the snow for over five minutes.

I jumped back on board and did my harness up but felt as though I had drunk 10 pints, so Fryster came to check it for me. Ramp up and off we went, descending through the beautiful mountains back to our little base called Ram Ram just outside Marrakech. Once we landed and shut down, I set to work. I had also cut the tops off four water bottles with my trusty Leatherman to make some little 'cocktail' glasses for us. By the time DC crewed out of the cockpit and made it down to the ramp, I was there with four drinks ready to go. Southern Comfort and orange juice, with freshly squeezed limes and of course Atlas Mountain Ice to finish it off. We toasted DC and his awesome career on Chinooks and threw a few snowballs around with the remaining snow from the ice box. It was hilarious as the other crews walked past in the 40-degree heat to crew into their aircraft and there we were, drinking cocktails and having a snowball fight. Definitely a 'Carlsberg moment'.

One of the other places we routinely visited looking for dust was Jordan. Thankfully, the Movenpick hotel in Aqaba was light years better than the Sangho with far less risk of seeing the contents of your stomach on a regular basis. It was so nice in fact it had its own ice cream shop, lovely bar and restaurant and private beach. This was situated on the shores of the Dead Sea and led to a fabulous view of the largest Jordanian flag I have ever seen flying on a pole that had to have been around 500ft tall. This was done as a clear display of defiance to the Israelis across the water. I cannot recommend swimming in the Dead Sea if you have forgotten to pack your goggles by the way, but apart from salty eyes I had little to complain about in Jordan. Unlike Marrakech, however, we weren't allowed to leave the hotel as there was a higher risk of hostile locals with objections to the British military operating on their soil. But similar to Marrakech there were plenty of belly dancers in the evenings for entertainment at the hotel. I had really embraced the belly-dancing culture in Morocco (not literally may I add) as women there seemed to have so much more freedom of choice. Morocco had been much more westernised, and the nightclubs and hotels had beautiful women wearing some stunning fashion, proudly able to show off their bodies and beauty. This cannot be said for Jordan. Nearly all the women in the hotel and on the beach were wearing burkas. Now I don't pretend to be an expert on the ins and outs of why they chose or indeed were forced to wear these, but I suspect it was the latter. On the beach they had swimming burkas that made them look like octopuses as they emerged from the water with the black material draped heavy with water around their silhouette from head to toe. They also would wear them at dinner time and that is when I picked up something that has stayed with me since. These cloaked women, walking shadows if you will, all had THE most amazing shoes on. Now it's well known that I love my heels and I was amazed at some of the designer offerings that I saw cladding these hidden figures' feet. Then it dawned on me. This was the only way these women could express themselves. The only way they could stand out from the next burka standing behind or beside them and the only way they could enjoy and indulge a little in what the rest of we females take for granted: freedom of choice. I loved seeing what they would step out in each night and would always give them a little nod at their shoes as they walked past me, and smile or wink. Their husbands would always be walking ahead of them as is customary so I knew I wouldn't cause the women misery with my subtle acknowledgement. I often wondered if they blushed behind their face coverings. But their eyes always gave it away as they creased at the edges and I knew they were smiling despite not seeing their grin, I knew they had appreciated my secret fashion high five! My life and their life were worlds apart. I had the choice of speech, an education, a job, and the clothes I wore, but we had one very important thing in common, Jimmy Choos and a love of Louboutin.

Finally, the Joint Helicopter Command in charge of us as a fleet and those that held the budget for our pre-deployment desert training saw sense and sent us out to El Centro to carry out our dust landing trainings. This was a huge United States Airforce Base situated in the middle of the Californian desert. The whole place was set up perfectly for training, with accommodation on camp and miles of desert along with 360-degree shooting ranges. This meant that for the first time ever we could fire all three weapons at once while training, which was the equivalent of a crewman's wet dream. We also had the Colorado River to fly low level down at 50ft. Sitting on the ramp waving at the Yanks having BBQs on their boats along the river was pure rockstar and would have been worthy of some Creedence Clearwater Revival soundtrack. But by far the best trips out here were the San Diego Heli lanes. We would fly through the city, past the USS *Midway* and along the sand of Pacific Beach, then up on to the millionaires' mansions before departing to the north-west. The final landmark to fly over, which of course had to be ticked off the bucket list, was Miramar airbase where the famous *Top Gun* movie was filmed. The Yanks had more aircraft on the deck at Miramar than the whole of the UK forces had between them, and it was an impressive sight to behold. Of course, a day of this had to be followed by a night stop in San Diego where we all made a point of visiting the 'Top Gun' bar for some cheesy photos and singing, *You've Lost that Loving Feeling*. Aircrew at their finest!

So, I have seen some great places around the world other than just dusty places and war zones. But my favourite city to fly over will always be London. We are extremely privileged as a force to be allowed to fly through the London Heli lanes when we request to do so for training purposes. There are many routes headed in from east to west and north to south but the main one we tend to follow is H3 that runs mostly along the Thames from Barnes to the Isle of Dogs. This route takes in the Houses of Parliament, London Eye, St Pauls, Canary Wharf and the O2 dome, obviously flying over the many beautiful bridges as we go. I've loved seeing the London skyline change over the years and seeing buildings such as the Shard and the Walkie-Talkie building pop up and alter the most distinctive skyline I've ever flown over. By far this sortie was done best at the end of a day's training when we were flying home back to Odiham, east to west. Sitting on the ramp, seeing the sights appear under your feet and waving to the people at their desks in the high-rise Canada One building and in the pods of the London Eye. And watching the orange ring glow around the city like a lasso as the sun slipped away and the evening traffic on the M25 built up. You can travel the world but there really is no place like home. Or at least Odiham and the south of England, as it was, by now, where my heart belonged.

There is one place that we routinely deployed to that was neither a dusty war zone nor a nice place: The Boat. The Boat was the term we used for almost any deployment embarked with the Royal Navy. Crews before me went to HMS *Illustrious* in her time, affectionately known as 'Lusty', and my era went to HMS *Ocean*, affectionately known as ... well, let's not go there. Now The Boat is a 'unique' experience. There was a real mix of emotion regarding how we were made to feel once on board. The main vibe was that the ship's company, i.e. those permanently on board, hated us being there, interfering with their daily routine, eating their food, and drinking their beer and mostly annoying them by asking where the toilets were? The reply always came 'the heads' are etc. Heads is the naval term for toilets, and it used to really get their goat when we referred to them as toilets. So, we made a point of it ALWAYS! This funny little battle went on for weeks when we were embarked, often asking the same cantankerous old navy matelot, who knew by this stage we were just trying to wind him up, and therefore sent us in the wrong direction. This was pretty easy considering most of us spent the majority of a three-week embarkation lost or walking around in circles. I say circles as there are two decks on HMS *Ocean* that go the whole way around the ship's circumference, 2 deck and 5 deck; the other decks are a series of little corridors going across the ship, with compartments for accommodation or crew rooms. Once you were in the depths of the ship you didn't know which end you were even facing – the front or the back – another term that used to piss the navy off as it's the bow and the stern according to them. I often found myself so lost that I ended up in the padre's little chapel via a set of climbing stairs through a hatch, definitely lost now (ha-ha!).

I spent the three weeks prior to my first marathon embarked on board HMS *Ocean*. This resulted in me having to continue my training while on board, running on one of the four treadmills placed around the ship. They were set in little alcoves off the main corridors and you had to book a much-sought-after slot for each day. Because these treadmills were placed across the ship rather than facing forward your running training took on the list of the ship. Depending on the sea state you found yourself either screaming downhill as fast as your legs could go or climbing what felt like Everest as the ship listed the other way. The bigger the sea state, the better the training! This could also be said for the spin bikes on board: you were either climbing Mount Ventoux or pedalling like Tim Peake as your body became weightless. By my second embarkation though I had become a salty sea dog and could find my way around the ship fairly easily after one revolution of getting lost again to get my bearings. It occurred to me just how foreign an environment it can be to those who have never been on board, when I went back as an instructor. I told the student crewman to stack all the kit we had in the cabin on the ramp as I went off to check in with the engineers. When I returned to the aircraft, all the bags had been neatly stacked to the roof on the ramp of our Chinook. What I had meant was the 'ramp' of the aircraft carrier that is then lowered like a lift into the belly of the ship and takes smaller helicopters, along with troops and kit, in and out of the hangar. A lesson for me as the instructor. In the words of Atticus Finch *'no one's born knowing, everyone's gotta learn'*. I never took anything for granted with my students' knowledge after that.

Chapter 11

The Mighty 'Wokka'

I could not write this book without a love letter to the aircraft that stole my heart back at the age of 17. The Chinook has a unique effect on everyone who flies in it and who works with this awesome helicopter. You can't not fall in love with it. Most people refer to an aircraft as 'her' in the female form, I have never attached this pronoun to the Chinook. Maybe because I am female or maybe just because it's a beast of an aircraft. The troops refer to it as 'the sound of freedom'. I guess that's because when they hear it coming, they know it's their chariot home or it's coming to rescue them from hell. I also refer to it in the same way when I hear its rhythm of thump, thump, thump far in the distance, and for me it meant a different freedom. The freedom from life, from mundane worries, from everyday bullshit and from an ordinary existence. When you are airborne nothing else matters but that Chinook bubble that you are floating in. The other stresses and woes of life fade away. It will always feel like home to me after so many hours spent in this familiar and comforting lump of rotating metal. The first thing you notice when you climb on board is the smell. The distinctive sweet smell of OM15 which is the hydraulic fluid. This smell always lingers somewhere, especially around the aft transmission area above your head as you walk up the ramp. But you learn to know what the 'normal' aroma is, verses when it spikes your 'Spidey' senses, and you know there's a more sinister leak somewhere. That's something that you can only get with experience on this beast, the 'feel' for when something is 'not quite right' and the older you get the more attuned you become to things that are amiss. There's a saying about the Chinook that if it isn't leaking oil somewhere then that's when you should be concerned as the sumps are empty. The smell of OM15 will stay with me forever. It was my perfume for so many years and lingered on my flying suit for hours after I stepped off the aircraft; it's engrained in my memory forever.

The other thing that was so familiar was the noise of crewing in. If someone played this back to me now, I would know without the need for any voices what was happening. The thud, thud, thud as you walk up the hollow metal ramp before you hit the reinforced floor area where the metal thuds continued but became more solid as you made your way up into the cabin. Then dropping all your flying kit, which you had lugged out on to one of the red side wall seats. These held a tension as they were all zipped together so there was always an inevitable 'boing' noise as your kit hit the seat, like an over-tensioned trampoline. Then depending on what the sortie was and whether you would need the centre hook or not would come the click, click of the two metal latches being opened before the loud bang as you lifted the access hatch and flipped it open, hitting the floor as it landed. I always used to tell students off for this as it should be opened carefully and 'placed' on the floor before it gets strapped down, but they never did. And in order to open the lower door to allow the hook to swing freely you had to use a little ratchet tool to release the locking ports on the lower door. These made a metal pop noise as they sprang out of the locked position, and you would hear the lower hatch door drop under its own weight just a few inches. Finally, you had to use the ratchet to wind the door open as it retracted back underneath the belly of the aircraft. You could tell it was in the correctly stored position, which was also ever so slightly different on each airframe, as the torque ratchet would click over and over, i.e., you had reached maximum tension. Again, a uniquely Chinook sound.

Walk rounds completed and cabin prepped we would all get our helmets on and the next noise that you heard was the bell, fixed to the ramp, but activated by a switch in the cockpit. This bell was rung before the pilots started the Auxiliary Power Unit (APU). Without the APU, which is effectively a little engine, you couldn't spin the rest of the mighty Wokka into life. It was like the jump lead that allowed every other system to follow on. The bell was a shrill bell, not like one you would press in a shop to get attention but more like an old house bell. It went right through you but made everyone nearby aware you were about to start up and things were about to get noisy. If we crewmen were still chatting down the back, waiting for the pilots to sort their lives out, it was the nod for us to stop gossiping and put our helmets on! First there was a whoosh as stored hydraulic pressure was sent to the starter motor of the system and you would hear the little APU wind itself up. It would get to 90 per cent rotation speed then click over to a higher pitch as it transitioned from a motor to a pump and was self-sufficient. The APUs were temperamental. They were old, as were most of the aircraft. Some of the older ones would take longer to get to this high-pitched whine. They laboured their way there and we as a crew would be willing it on for a few seconds before we heard the distinctive change of tone as it became self-sufficient, and you knew it was working properly. After a while, crews began to know which aircraft had APUs that were slightly older around the fleet, especially on deployment as we flew the same aircraft regularly. What was funny though is when you were listening to an aircraft, not your own, start up and you heard the APU wind itself up, then promptly wind itself down. Doh! This usually meant that aircraft was not going anywhere. Or that the start system needed repressurising which meant the crewman having to frantically pump a large metal handle on the ramp to pressurise the 'bomb', a black cylinder above your head holding the pressure. This activity always meant getting a sweat on and was shared between the two crewmen taking turns if you were lucky or the ground crew as well if they were around to step in. Your heart would sink if it was you that was standing as the No.1 crewman below a lacklustre APU as you knew what was coming. You would pump the handle for a few minutes – especially fun wearing all your kit and body armour in 45 degrees – as the pilots watched in their mirror from the cockpit chuckling, before giving it another attempt. Everyone kept their fingers crossed for the second attempt as if this failed, they ALL knew what was coming. If it did not start this time, it was broken – which meant one of two things. You either weren't going anywhere OR you would be crewing into the spare aircraft. Now although this gave the option to still get flying, having to lug all your kit to a second aircraft, do another walk around, get the centre hook out etc. and mostly under time pressure was unanimously agreed by the whole force as the most hateful thing. Sometimes you almost hoped there wasn't a spare so you could just head back into the crew room for a brew. And it seemed like a cruel joke, planned by the engineers, but the spare aircraft for the day was usually parked the furthest away from the broken one you were standing on! So off we went lugging our helmets, aircrew jacket, crewman tool kit, nav bag, flight rations, NVG (Night Vision Goggles), a large torch and, if you were deployed, your SA80 weapon, go bag of bullets and a cooler box. You get the idea …

If the APU start was successful, the rest of the start sequence would begin. It's amazing how I still remember this so many years after I last flew. I still think I could go back now and carry out an aircraft start with no hiccups. It was like following a little song or dance and became engrained in you where to stand and what to do for each check, without even thinking. I used to pride myself on making this as slick as possible and being ahead at every step, ready to reply as the pilots prompted the system check. But the start also involved all the senses, again a learnt skill that came with experience. You would watch the pressure indicator and the rotor blades during the hydraulic checks for surges in pressure or a discrepancy in their movement. You would listen to the first engine spin up as you stood beneath it announcing when it too, like the APU, had reached the 'good start' point. You would do the same for the second engine, but you couldn't hear this engine as by then the blades had begun to rotate. Instead, you would place your hand against the airframe below the engine and you could 'feel' it spin up as it vibrated through the metal. All the while subconsciously having your eyes, ears and nose engaged for anything out of the ordinary. The more experienced you got, the more niggles you could pick up, such as a grinding noise from the transmissions, a slightly stronger smell of fuel, a centre hook that took too long to close properly. I came to know that aircraft better than any car I ever drove. Like a mum who knows her children, I could tell when something was up, when something wasn't quite right, and the aircraft was out of sorts.

The Chinook is an aircraft that wants to be operated. Flying around the sky empty without purpose felt as unfulfilling for me as I'm sure it did for it. It's a battlefield helicopter and this is where it thrives. I think that is why I loved being deployed so much as this is when we got to use the aircraft to its full potential. Routinely filling the cabin with as much payload as we could fit in and when we ran out of space inside, sticking what was left on the hooks beneath. This is when as a crewman you earned your money, making the plan as how best to achieve maximum capability. Weighing up what is better to go inside, or in a net under slung. The bigger bulkier things took up more space in the cabin but sometimes were too light to under sling. And some of the heavier loads we were presented either wouldn't fit inside or if they could, would break the floor loading limits. We had to know every limit and characteristic of how certain loads would fly. As a rule of thumb, the heavier and denser something was the better it would fly as a USL. The lighter and bigger things always flew like a nightmare. I still remember one task to recover a Reaper, which was an unmanned aircraft that had crash-landed in the red desert. This particular drone was shaped just like a mini aircraft not like the helicopter-shaped ones you see around today. We picked it up on a strop attached to our centre hook and off we went. This thing was designed to be aerodynamic, which resulted in it trying to fly itself every time we increased the speed above 40 knots. The blooming thing would regularly appear at the ramp as it swung on the long strop, and once again only experience taught you when enough was enough and to slow down and reduce the swing to an acceptable level.

As I mentioned above, the Chinook is a battlefield helicopter. It's used to getting shot at and almost designed for that purpose. I have taken numerous rounds pepper-potted around the aircraft and still managed to make it back to Bastion with all systems working. That's the bonus with us being so large; although we present a bigger target for the enemy to aim at, there is more redundant space around the aircraft so the enemy would have to be doing well to hit something vital. This was different from the Puma, Lynx and many other smaller helicopters who have all their important flying systems concentrated into one area. The blades of the Chinook are titan-like. I've seen them slice through trees and remain undamaged, indeed a good pilot friend of mine has part of a tree that he trimmed with a blade going into a confined area, mounted on his wall at home. He certainly made the clearing large enough to fit in after the incident and his wife was a genius for getting the lads from the squadron to recover the branch before presenting it to him as a gift. I've seen a foot and a half be taken off a blade by enemy fire and it remain turning, all be it the ride home was a little bumpier. The Chinook has two engines so if one packs up the other can take over. We have redundancy for nearly every system on that aircraft and we are all trained in emergency drills so we can deal with most things that could go wrong. That said, in all my years flying I was very lucky and had no massive catastrophic system failures. As long as those blades are still turning that aircraft can get you on the ground safely, even without the engines working, as the pilots are trained to autorotate to land. This is basically where the pilot uses his skill – yes, they do have some – to adjust the angle of the blades so they maintain their centrifugal force and continue to spin, providing an element of control. Autorotating is a last resort to land a helicopter that has lost engine power; it requires the pilot to lower the collective lever to flatten the blade angle therefore make them spin faster and maintain momentum, but they must balance this carefully with not letting the blades overspeed. Imagine a ballerina spinning with her arms out, the speed of her hands is far faster than her body is rotating and therefore they want to raise up. Clearly this would be very bad indeed if our blades did the same. To prevent this happening and the blades coning to meet each other at the top, the handling pilot raises his collective lever a touch to slow them down to within RPM (rotations per minute) range. They manage and adjust this the whole way to the surface, much of it is judged through listening to the blades as they get faster as well as watching the RPM gauge while the co-pilot sings out the RPM shown on the dial. You can hear them from the cabin and shout NR which is basically rotation speed if he hasn't noticed them getting faster. We work as a team, but the handling pilot ultimately has the control, and we have a saying on the force, no stick no vote, which in itself is controversial except for this circumstance when he is fully responsible for your little pink body surviving. Thankfully, only one aircraft has ever had to do this for real and it was the squadron boss at the time. He landed successfully in the desert in Iraq and all the crew walked away to tell the tale. The mighty Wokka has saved me and my friends more times than I can count and ironically, despite being the closest I have ever been to death while on board the aircraft, it's where I have always felt safest.

My favourite noise, however, is this: hearing the APU wind down as we shut down at the end of a day's tasking. It's so distinctive as it goes in reverse from its high-pitched whine to silence as this time it is being closed down. Almost like a vacuum cleaner when you switch it off, the noise ebbs away and all you are left with is the noise of the casing crackling with heat residue as it settles itself back to sleep. Then it's time for helmets off which is usually accompanied by a gasp or groan at the end of a long warm day's tasking. We as crewmen then set about putting the cabin back to how it should look, a place for everything and everything in its place. There's an unwritten rule that you should always leave a cabin in the way you expect to find it, otherwise you are just screwing over the next crewmen who come to crew in. This husbandry entails: putting any USL strops neatly to one side for the engineers to do their post use inspection; lengthening all the seat belts that have been used and tightened up around skinny soldiers or cadets; and popping any restraint equipment used away. Lastly hanging up your 'monkey' harness – the ones we had worn around our waists to keep us attached to the aircraft – and the hateful task of untangling your interrupter cable. These were long wiggly comms leads that we plugged into our helmets so we could also walk freely around the cabin while remaining on the intercom. They appeared to have minds of their own and a love affair with themselves. If the lead could entwine its cable around any other part of its spring it would do so the second you weren't looking. It also had a fetish for vehicle mirrors, troop Bergens and exposed radio antennae, attaching itself to them within seconds of being in close proximity. Finally, it was time to gather your kit and head out over the ramp, always making sure someone switched the battery off from a panel on the left-hand side of the exterior of the aircraft. The battery on the Chinook was about as much use as a chocolate fireguard and was well known for running down in minutes if not switched off fairly sharpish after shutting down. Whoever switched it off would call, 'battery's off' so everyone knew this essential task had been done. Many times, we have boarded a crew bus, or been standing back in an Ops tent when someone on the crew pipes up with 'who did the battery?' Even if you knew it was you, doubt always crept in, like when you leave for holiday and wonder if you switched the iron off, or locked the front door. It was, of course, forgotten the odd time by crews which resulted in them and the aircraft being stuck somewhere until a new battery could be sent out. For some reason this always seemed to occur in unusually sunny, bustling destinations such as Ibiza or Nice, must have been the heat that distracted the crew!

Once the battery was safely off it was back in for tea 'and medals' usually wandering in as a crew. I hated leaving anyone alone to lug their kit back in all by themselves, unless of course I needed a tinkle then all bets were off. We regularly bantered other crews as we all walked across the flight dispersal, back to the squadron from a deliberate op or formation sortie. When airborne it was game on to banter each other but on the deck, it was crew brothers in arms vs the other aircrafts' crew.

This whole process begins with the APU and ends with it winding down. That noise is a sign of the end. The end of your amazing flying adventure; the end of your high adrenaline troop insert that you survived; the end of an emergency but you made it back to base; the end of a MERT shout recovering injured soldiers; and sometimes the end of a life, of the casualty who didn't make it and was to be loaded off in silence and with dignity. The Chinook is the most amazing aircraft in the world in my humble opinion, however, it's the people that breathe life into this beautiful lump of metal that make her glow. Each and every engineer that painstakingly takes her apart and lovingly puts her back together again. The engineers that stay up throughout the cold nights to fix her ready for morning and another day's tasking. And of course, the aircrew who strap themselves into her every sortie and fly her to the best of her ability to save lives and recover soldiers. They are all heroes in my eyes.

Chapter 12

Time to Start a Life

In 2014, the British Forces were to pull out of Helmand and hand Camp Bastion back to the Afghans. A lot of time was spent on my last deployment helping to enable the Chinook fleet to withdraw back to Kandahar before a final move up north to Kabul. It was definitely time to say goodbye to this war zone as over the years there had been more and more 'red tape' as we call it arriving in theatre. We had gone from the early days where we were left to our own devices, and no one cared if you had your beret on to a world of 'hat police' and being ordered to wear high visibility belts when walking around Camp Bastion. These belts were brought in to prevent people being run over around camp at night. I had a theory on this, if you were there to fight a war and therefore deemed able to dodge bullets and fight an enemy then surely you should be capable of not getting run over by your own troops in the dark. The sad fact is that rules like this only come into force after an incident which means that some numpty had indeed been run over by a vehicle around camp. This I could only put down to natural selection or maybe his mates just wanted rid of him. When we arrived at Bastion in 2006 it was a barbed wire fence, we had one Land Rover, with no doors or a windscreen. This was because when we had to get to the aircraft rapidly for a call-out we abandoned it at the side of the HLS. Every time we made an approach over it to land on again, the Landy would get blasted by our downwash and the doors would blow open and bang on their hinges until they were warped beyond repair, and the windscreen would get pebble-dashed and shattered, so it was easier just to remove them.

But it was a vehicle and we needed something to carry our copious amounts of kit between the flight line and the aircraft. We very rarely had the use of any 'wheels' to get ourselves around camp so most of our working day was spent walking along the dusty road between our accommodation and the Ops tents. By 2014, there were senior officers rolling around in their airconditioned white hi-luxes while the rest of us faced getting charged for not wearing seatbelts in our worn-out Land Rovers if they saw us. The more of these rules that came into force the more painful life on detachment became, with an abundance of senior brass coming out to get their Herrick medal before we withdrew. I think having seen it from its infancy as a proper war zone and seeing the lads fighting and living in the FOBs made it all the more difficult to swallow some of the 'rules to make war look pretty' as it wasn't, and that's a fact. Bastion became its own little bubble of rules and regulations and we and the true 'wardogs' hated it. I remember landing from one MERT shout and running into the Ops tent for an update on the intelligence before we were due to lift for more tasking. I ripped my flying helmet off my head and stood waiting for the intel update with stains of blood on my flying kit and a face covered in sweat and dust. Some senior female officer walked past me and said, 'can you please put your hair in a bun, it's not supposed to be touching your collar.' It took all my strength not to swing for her. Most definitely time to leave.

I remember the last day on shift out there. I left the MERT tent and headed out to the blast wall beside where we slept and wrote a little poem in black marker on its concrete face, signed off as Gloria Stitz, my pseudonym. Sadly, my poem, along with all the amazing artwork on the blast walls painted by each section was not to survive as all the blast walls would be whitewashed before Bastion was handed back to the Afghan army. I saw a documentary on British Forces TV recently of how Bastion looked now and it was like having a tour around the Mary Celeste, I recognised parts of the camp but it just looked like an abandoned old fairground. That last day, we flew back to Kandahar and completed our final hand over to 27 Squadron who would be moving the force up to Kabul. Their crews in turn flew us back to Bastion a few days later to catch the fixed wing C17 aircraft back to the UK. As I sat there, now a passenger, I was tinged with emotion. Op Herrick had been the best of times and the worst of times, but it had given me purpose. Bastion had become almost as familiar a place to me as my home in the UK. It was the simple life, eat, sleep, fly, repeat and the normal worries we face in life slide away when you are in that bubble of deployment. My mate, Dan, a pilot, was sitting next to me and he showed me a photo of his little boy as we lifted and smiled. We had all deployed there as young adults back in 2006 and now – eight years later and my tenth and final deployment now done – how life had changed so much. We used to enjoy getting back to the UK to hit the pubs and go on holiday, but now so many of us just wanted to get home to kids and families, or something as simple as walking around barefoot on carpet. As we lifted, I looked out of the ramp at the warm air, the engines throw-out, mixing in with the desert air forming the haze I was so used to seeing. I slid my dark visor down so no one could see the tears forming in my eyes. Searching the emotions that I was feeling, I realised I was sad that it was over, not relieved, sad. A part of me will always remain in Helmand.

Over the years we spent away, there was this thing happening back here called 'life'. Yep, it hadn't stopped every time we were away for months on end, it just carried on without us. I had missed best mates' weddings, family gatherings, Christmases, and birthday parties. Finally, I could start to say yes to things rather than 'I'm away on that date.' It also meant Skelfy and I could finally spend some time together as a proper couple. We had both been away so much over the years, the worst being a full calendar year when we only saw one another a total of four weeks in twelve months as he was in Iraq and I was in Afghanistan. We had managed one holiday in nine years, so we booked to go to New York on my return from this last deployment. The first place we visited was the 9/11 museum. It was haunting, walking around it. That fateful day we both remember so well and a day that had shaped both our lives in the forces and ironically had resulted in our paths crossing in Iraq. We had planned to go to this museum first thing then spend the day sightseeing as most would do in our shoes. After we walked out of the place though, all we wanted to do was head to the pub. We managed to find an Irish bar near to the 9/11 site. Irish bars are usually not my preferred choice may I add, but this one was special. It had a scrapbook on the bar of pictures of all the fallen firefighters from ladder house 10 which was the first on scene. It was a lovely way to raise a glass to the fallen heroes. On our penultimate morning in NYC, we had planned to go for a run in Central Park. We both loved our running and thought it would be a good box to tick while there. I, however, was hungover from the night before and really did not want to go. Skelfy dragged me out of bed and said we had brought our trainers all this way and we were going, a fact which I couldn't argue with! Reluctantly I pulled my trainers on, knowing it would probably clear my head, and I would regret not going in the long run, excuse the pun.

It was November and a beautiful crisp sunny Sunday, with runners everywhere. Central Park was just around the corner from our hotel on 99th Street. It is massive, and we just wound our way around all the little paths and lakes getting lost and for once not timing ourselves. At one point, Skelfy stopped to 'tie his shoelace'. He was taking ages so eventually I turned round to say, 'hurry up you mincer' as was our usual way, and he was holding a silver ring up. 'This was in my shoe.' The ring looked just like one of mine and my first thought was it had dropped into his trainer from the messy pile of jewellery I had left on the bedroom table at the hotel. I thought he was about to go mad at me for giving him a blister. He followed the initial statement up with, 'You've put up with me for this long, shall we do it?' I was so shocked, as Skelfy and I had the mentality that, 'If it ain't broke don't fix it'. We almost made a point of saying we would never get married and he had been married previously and always said never again. I looked at him in bewilderment and asked, 'Is this a joke?' He laughed and exclaimed 'NO! Don't leave me hanging.' It was the most romantic and surprising moment of my life. I said yes and we ran back to the hotel grinning like idiots with my new engagement ring on under my gloves, announcing like a giddy teenager to the staff on the way past reception that we had just got engaged. Now it turns out that Skelfy had been planning this for some time. He had asked my dad for permission while I was in Afghanistan, and both sets of parents knew he planned to ask me in New York. He was also so nervous he had asked a few of our mates how to do it; seems as if the only person who had NO idea was me! We got showered and off we went to celebrate, but the first thing we had to find was a chemist for blister plasters. Nope, Skelfy hadn't got a blister running with my ring in his shoe, but he had clearly sized it from one of my bigger rings back home. The ring on my engagement finger would have fitted my big toe it was that large, but I was adamant I was wearing it. After a surprisingly difficult mission on a Sunday in New York we found some plasters that I put around it to wedge it on my finger discreetly so I could still show it off. I loved it so much and kept admiring it as we sat sipping champagne on a rooftop bar. Skelfy eventually burst out laughing and informed me it was in fact a 'stunt ring' and only cost £60 from the 'Elizabeth Duke' catalogue. He had bought it purely for the proposal moment until I had a chance to pick my own on returning to the UK. The funny bit though, our best mate, who went on to be our best man told him, 'Mate if she doesn't suss, I would just let her keep it.' Cheapskate. Skelfy wouldn't let me, and as soon as we got home, we had one designed and made, obviously it had to be a Tiffany design as a special nod to New York City.

Now my first words on discussing when to get married was that we couldn't do it next summer as I had an 'event' in my calendar for that year. I and my crew gal mates Anna and Becs had signed up to complete an Iron Man triathlon in 2015. I had done a few sprint tri's before but nothing like going straight in at the deep end, after a drunken pinkie promise at one of our BBQs. For those that don't know, an Iron Man consists of a 2.4-mile open water swim, 112-mile bike ride, finished off with a full marathon, yep 26.2 miles. I bought a new road bike and wetsuit and threw myself into training. I would cycle to work, run at lunchtime and finish with a swim almost daily. However, the first time I got in the lake to try open water swimming can only be summed up as horrendous. I basically drowned in a forward motion until I made it to the first buoy. Becs was with me as I stopped for air. On surfacing and coughing up copious amounts of water, I almost broke down in tears. I just couldn't do it; despite being such a good swimmer I found it impossible. She looked at me and said, 'You're probably holding your breath, just remember to breathe.' Off I went, slightly more successfully down the back stretch of the lake stopping less and less in a childlike panic as I went. As I swam, I repeated the mantra 'just breathe, just breathe, just breathe'. The next loop of the lake I did without stopping and never looked back. I got these words tattooed on the inside of my wrist before the Iron Man and I routinely glance down at them when I'm in a stressful situation and, well, 'just breathe'. Sounds simple but sometimes we all forget.

I loved that summer of training for this event known as the Outlaw. Skelfy didn't really run or swim so he joined me on many of my long bike rides and we would often stop at the local on the way home on a summer's evening for an isotonic beer and cider. The day of the event sadly wasn't quite so blissful. We started in the lake in Nottingham at 0600 and then upon exiting the lake just over an hour later it began to rain. And it rained, and it rained. Now coming from Northern Ireland I'm fairly used to what we know as Irish sunshine and I pride myself on being fairly robust, but this weather was another level. It turned what should have been a fun day enjoying the months of hard training, into a test of mental tenacity that no amount of training could have prepared me for. Or maybe I was wrong. I look back at that day and how tough it was just to keep going, feeling useless as my hands and feet froze on the bike and I limped my way through puddles in soaking wet kit to complete the marathon all the way into the dark. But I'm utterly convinced that an unwavering tenacity came from somewhere within me. Was it always there from basic training or did the A course teach me it? Every so often I see glimpses of this inner steel and surprise even myself at my refusal to give up.

Iron Man completed, it was now time to focus on the wedding planning for the following summer and of course the hen do. Now here's the thing, 90 per cent of my mates at the time were lads from work. A mix of crewmen and pilots, old and young, pretty boys, and hairy lads. So, what did I decide to do? Oh yes, have a 'drag' do instead. We hired a party bus from the main gate at RAF Odiham that took me, the hen, and my twenty-seven men down to Brighton for a night. We had THE best fun and will still go down in history as one of the best nights out I've ever had. They all made such an effort and some of them scrubbed up surprisingly well in miniskirts and heels. The toilet stop on the way to Brighton was the highlight of the evening though when one of the lads bumped into his mother-in-law while dressed in a red wig, mini dress and heels on the way to the men's toilets where the rest of the lads where now lined up with their skirts hitched up to take a leak! That picture will make me laugh till the day I die! When it came to wedding-dress shopping, I can't say I really enjoyed it much. I'm a shopaholic usually but the whole bridezilla thing just wasn't me. I went on my own, so I didn't have to share my trauma with my gal pals, and with my only requirements being no lace and no flouncy meringues. I found one pretty early on, job done. My closest friends thought I may have steered away from the normal white wedding dress and there was much discussion around this subject between them all. We decided the theme for the wedding to be red, white, and blue with lots of patriotic nods to our time in the forces. As our guests arrived, they had to take either a red, white or blue helium-filled balloon from Anna and Claire who were holding the bunch at the door, to match the colour they thought I would be wearing, a red dress, a white dress or blue for a military

(MTP) patterned dress. The guest list was a mix of Hereford SAS soldiers and RAF Odiham Chinook crews with a lovely sprinkling of Northern Irish and Yorkshire friends and family. Skelfy arrived in a Scout helicopter on to the green outside the bar as our guests watched on and we had an SAS flag flying above the hotel. All like the scene out of a movie really. Grohly was my 'bridesman' and walked, no in fact, danced ahead in a dapper red three-piece suit with my other bridesmaid Jussy in her lovely matching red dress. As my dad and I walked around the corner towards the outside 'Folly', I was greeted with a sea of the mixed balloons. I laughed at just how many red and blue balloons there were as I walked towards Skelfy in my fairy-tale white dress holding my bouquet made from British Legion paper poppies. After we'd said 'I do', our guests all released their balloons to the sky, and two of our best mates played *Dakota* by the Stereophonics on their guitars. The top table had a massive Union Jack draped over it and I had made my own decorations for the tables with poppies wrapped in ribbons made from my old combats. The whole day had such a great military theme, but the highlight was the field phones we had wired to all the tables so each table could call their mates on another table for a chat. It was fabulous, rowdy chaos. We catered the night do with a pizza wagon and a Krispy Kreme stack rather than a wedding cake. And my brothers and mates were last seen heading outside to play 'human Jenga' at 0300. I must admit 13 August 2016 was an awesome day and I still look back on it and smile. Once again though, my aptitude for taking or getting pictures to capture the day was lacking but I have the fond memories tucked away for safe keeping.

No rest for the wicked, however, and later that year on Boxing Day off I went to the Falklands for another deployment. The first New Year's Eve as man and wife and I was deployed. The irony. This time down south was a completely different vibe. The military had closed many of the section bars indefinitely and clamped down on excessive drinking. We were on standby nearly the whole time as well so couldn't drink, regardless. This was probably a blessing in disguise as I spent most of my time in the gym or in the Olympic-size swimming pool. My neck had been playing up for nearly a year now having had a career wearing a flying helmet, often fitted with night vison goggles while hanging out of the belly of a helicopter. But I had managed to limp through with the help of lots of painkillers and physio. I passed my 3,000 hours flying mark while in the Falklands which is a significant milestone, then about a week later my neck gave up for good. I came home from the Falklands barely able to turn my head and felt as if I was attached to a crucifix. I didn't know at the time that my last flight operating on a Chinook would be flying a Land Rover USL out to Mount Alice at 40 knots on a Friday night. I began my Chinook flying career with a Falklands detachment and sadly ended it with one fourteen years later. I arrived back at Odiham to enter the rehabilitation system to try and get me back in the air. I found myself at Headley Court, the centre of excellence for injured service personnel, and a place that had been instrumental in putting so many of the injured soldiers I had collected back together. Headley Court was an amazing place, although no longer exists. This I guess is a good thing as Headley Court existed in its heyday with the sole purpose of helping our wounded servicemen to get back on their feet, sometimes literally. When I arrived on its doorstep in 2017, I was living in the block for the entirety of my course. There were loads of empty rooms and walking around in the evenings it felt like a ghost town. I was informed though that at one time, every single room on camp was occupied, with a waiting list for people to attend courses. This was an eye-opener for me once again as although I had rescued many of our injured soldiers, this was the pinch point they all came through. The idea of each of the hundreds of rooms being filled with our broken and limbless guys and girls really hit me. Sadly, not even the experts here could fix my neck enough to enable me to put the weight of a flying helmet back on it. I was broken, my flying days were over for good. In finally accepting this I don't know which hurt more, my neck or my heart.

Chapter 13

The Essence of a Crewman

I am a Chinook crewman. I did not just do it as a job, I became it through and through in every fibre of my being. I can't pinpoint exactly when I felt the distinct change from it just being a role in the RAF to my raison d'etre. I had chased the dream of becoming 'that' since I was 17 and had achieved it and woven it into my DNA. There are few people who will ever make it as a Chinook crewman. We are a unique bunch, both physically and mentally, so it's ironic that by the end of our careers both of these are usually broken. It is possibly one of the hardest jobs to explain to people as to what it entails but I hope that thus far I have given you some insight. Sadly, it's not a job you can transition your skill set easily into civvy street when you leave the military unlike a pilot can. And the hardest challenge of my career was finally admitting that I could no longer be a crewman.

It was around the 15-year mark of my career I began to develop upper neck pain. Lots of crewmen have neck and back injuries due to the positions we find ourselves in and heavy kit that we wear, especially on our heads for night flying. I kept ignoring my pain and continued to fly through it, while also training for the Iron Man triathlon. One day, walking in from a sortie, my other crewmate Spence asked me something from behind. I turned my full body to answer him, and he instantly scolded me. 'Liz, go to the flipping physio FFS.' I finally resigned myself to the fact that my neck was not getting any better and now I could barely look over my left and right shoulders without immense pain. I was grounded instantly by the doctor on station, as I knew would be the case, and immediately added to the physio rehabilitation system. Going to my weekly physio sessions was like an aircrew reunion as so many of my old mates were in exactly the same 'shit state' as we called it with their necks and backs. After a few months of intense physio, I managed to get myself signed off to fly again, but sadly this bliss didn't last long and just weeks later my pain resurfaced and I was grounded again. I couldn't let my career end like this, so I embraced a further round of physio and a strength and conditioning programme, knowing I was pencilled in to go back to the Falklands on Boxing Day for six weeks. That's the other thing about crewmen, we are such a band of brothers that we never shirk our scheduled deployments as you know one of your mates will have to go instead. Down in the Falklands if your replacement didn't make it on to their flight or they were delayed in any way, you had to stay in situ. We referred to this circumstance as being 'bennied' for some reason and I still have never got to the bottom of why. I couldn't face my colleague getting bennied for New Year's Eve, so I did everything in my power to get upgraded to fly in time to go. Despite still being in pain, I convinced the senior consultant at RAF Brize Norton that I was OK, and he reluctantly signed me back up as fit to fly, and a few weeks later off I went on the twelve-hour flight to Mount Pleasant Airbase, the Falklands.

As I mentioned, this deployment was much less boozy than my first deployment down there back in 2004. We were always holding standby for Search and Rescue cover despite being the most ridiculous aircraft for this role due to our downwash. But that meant less beer, more gym and meant for a much more 'memorable' time down there. The evening before our replacements landed into MPA we were tasked to take a USL across to West Falkland Island, to a site called Mount Alice. The USL flew at around 60 knots, so it took us an age to get it there and fly home. What a rock and roll Friday night as we finally crewed out, got a pizza as we had missed dinner and headed to bed. I woke up the next day feeling as if I was attached to a crucifix. I could barely move my neck or entire upper body. I headed straight

Basic Recruit 209 Course

Pass out parade, Cranwell

Above: Chinook OCF with Dave; side by side as always!

Below: Tent City, Basra

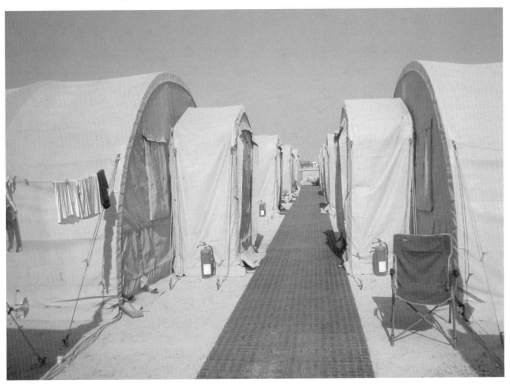

Pizzas with 27 Squadron and Roly, in Basra

The 'Camel's Toe' bar in Basra, two cans per night only!

R and R troops – just 24 honestly…

Christmas tasking

Op 'Certain Death', spot my mate Jonah the joker!

Holy oil from the American padre on the aircraft weapons

Liz's bullet hole!

Me and my sidekick Grohly after a hard day's work

Dear Afghanistan,

My mum once told me that everything in life is either a pleasure or an experience.....
   You have been both.

   Some of the best memories,
   Some of the worst.
   Sights I will never forget,
   Sights I wish I could.
   Commrades I have made forever
   Commrades I have lost.

   Too many beautiful sunrises,
   And one final sunset.

   Thanks for looking after me,
   Thanks for the memories.

                    Gloria
                         x

Above: Gloria's poem to Afghanistan on the blast wall before she left

Left: Gloria Stitz on my helmet badge. A part of me will always miss Gloria

to the physio who took one look at me and grounded me instantly. Thankfully, our replacements had arrived the day before so there was no impact on the tasking line, despite me being taken out of the crew plot. It was almost as if my body knew and it said, 'OK love, you have battled through enough of this now, no more, if you don't stop, I will make you.' Despite going to Headley Court and seeing numerous specialists, I never flew again.

After a few months of kicking my heels in frustration around the squadron, who had been amazing at looking after me, the station found me a desk job in headquarters. Initially, I accepted it as I was just glad to remain part of the team at Odiham, but I soon realised I was not, I straight away felt like a squadron outsider. Odiham is a huge hamster wheel that just keeps churning whether you are on the wheel or not. I missed being on 18 Squadron dreadfully as they were like my family and I would sit at my desk and stare out of the window at the aircraft hovering before departing on their daily adventures. I would watch them do circuit training with USLs and all I wanted was to be back up there in that cold, oily, smelly but beautiful, aircraft. A month later I made the hardest and scariest choice ever and took the option for a medical discharge to leave the service. Back into the civilian world that I had no idea about. I had joined up at such a young age, I had never really experienced 'real' life, without the stabilisers the RAF had provided me with. Honestly, this was the most daunting decision of my entire adult life, but the only one I felt I could make.

This is the part of the book where I want to try and explain exactly what a crewman is. We are practical, not educated and we are good at lunging. We had pilots who could work out the square root of a jam jar but couldn't take the lid off. The crewman would do that for them. We could think on our feet as the ramp went down and we were presented with a diverse load to try and fit into the aircraft cabin. Imagine playing a bad game of Tetris while getting shot at, that was us, making the cargo fit neatly together in a stack. We were inventive, especially when faced with a donkey to transport or the CO's car with his cat inside, or maybe even under slinging a cow free from being trapped in the mud. We were the eyes and ears of the pilot, safely voice marshalling the aircraft on to slopes, into small landing sites and on to ridges, and we were good at lunging. We were radio operators and navigators, especially when the pilot knew he was just about to get lost and would hand it to us 'crewman, your nav', knowing we would put him back on track.

We were party animals who were good at lunging. Our favourite sport, apart from lunging, was leading young pilots astray on a night out. But we were also babysitters, frequently entrusted with the same young pilots by the hierarchy to look after, which we did. Masters of fancy dress and offending people, mostly other crewmen's sisters and mums at summer balls. But we were also the best hosts and the most welcoming and charming individuals when we wanted to be, while not lunging. We hunted in packs and had one another's backs. When I referred to the mafia earlier, I wasn't joking, that's what it was like, the pilots used to warn one another not to upset the mafia. If we had your 'six' we had it, through thick and thin. If we didn't like you, goddamn you knew about it as the banter would stop. We only bantered the ones we liked.

But mostly we were aviators. We knew our trade and every inch of that aircraft. We could fix things that went wrong both on the ground and in the air and the pilots trusted our knowledge when offering advice in an emergency. We were the ones on the aircraft with the greatest capacity, mostly used up by lunging, and often saved the day with some essential radio information or task update that had been missed by the front end. We had the best seat in the house while seated on the ramp looking out. We worked the 'shop floor' and engaged with our passengers. Often the pilots couldn't see what was going on down the back, but it was our office to manage and lunge in. We were the defenders of our crew and passengers, entrusted with the weapons and the responsibility that comes with pulling the trigger. Ultimately 'if it's him or me, it's him', was my mantra, you knew when it was time to squeeze the trigger. But most importantly, we were the little voice of reason in the pilot's ear. We had no callsign so would never make decisions over the captain of the aircraft. He would always have the final say, but we had one sentence in our armour to save the aircraft from many a disaster … 'are you sure that's a good idea sir?'

Over the years, I had matured from being everyone's little sister whom they had to look after to their cool auntie they came to for advice, and then many years later the role of 'Mum'. 'Go speak to Liz' was a frequent phrase, as I had been around for so long. In fact, by the time I left, I almost felt like grandma with my knackered neck at the age of 36. Having become an instructor in 2010, it was a highlight to see some of my former students pass their Combat Ready checks and blossom as a crewman. I always tried to set a good example with my professional and personal conduct and kept my fitness in top peak. I was the only female crewman on the Chinook fleet for four years. I am still the longest-serving Chinook crew gal with over seventeen years' service under my belt, all of which was on the mighty Chinook. I never wanted to be a burden, so I made sure I was on top of my game at everything within my control. I was lucky enough to be selected as an Air Gunnery Instructor and later became a Qualified Helicopter Crewman Instructor. I loved teaching and seeing that lightbulb moment for my students when they achieved something. I think as a female in this role I was readily approachable, or at least I hope I was. And not being the most technically minded person, I always aimed to teach things in as simple and easily understandable manner as I could. My most frequently asked and least favourite question over the years was this: 'What challenges have you faced being a female in your role?' The truth, none. The crewmen never once made me feel as though I was an outsider or 'special' for being female. But I wasn't a trailblazer either, there were crew gals before me, and plenty came after me and will continue to do so. Although we refer to ourselves as crew gals, our job is 'crewman' and we wouldn't have it any other way. I hope that the crazy PC world we live in now never gets its teeth into this nametag. I was once involved in an all-female flypast in London, at the unveiling of the Women of War monument on Whitehall. We couldn't even gather a whole female crew of four, so it was just myself and Hannah, and for the purposes of the BBC commentator, Flight Lieutenant Glenda M. ... and Flight Sergeant Davina B. (i.e., Glen and Dave) ... and yes, we did manage to park it when we landed before you ask!

Anna and Bex came to visit 27 Squadron way back in 2004. Roly had entrusted them both to my supervision while they held on the squadron for a few weeks. I remember they were much more laddish than me and into football, which I was most definitely not. At the squadron footy that afternoon I recall feeling very lacking in ability and suddenly very girly and useless; a rubbish example to anyone with my lack of talent on the pitch! A few years later, both Anna and Bex joined us on the wing as crew gals and Anna said to me that I had inspired her to keep pushing for Chinooks as she saw that females could do the role just as well as males. I was bowled over as this was the first female I was able to do that for. A few years later 'little Becs' and Gemma arrived on to the fleet. Typical, five female crewmen now and two of them share the same name! Oh, and did I mention we were all blonde and had all been posted to 18 Squadron. A year or so later, Claire arrived to swell the numbers to a grand total of six. This was the only time in my twelve years on 18 Squadron that I had ever had to queue for the girls' toilet beside the crew room. What a novelty.

One morning in January 2016 Anna sent me an email. She would normally be sitting next to me in the briefing room but wasn't there, so I opened the email straight away as I already thought something was amiss. The email began, 'Dude I don't know how to tell you this face to face or via text so I'm emailing. Please don't tell anyone but I've been diagnosed with cancer' ... as I read it, the words genuinely jumped around on my phone. I got up and made my way out of the briefing room full of squadron personnel before the tears began to roll down my cheeks. I left the squadron and went straight to her house.

I walked into her kitchen and tried to hold it together, for her more than me, but we just both broke down in tears. She told me that the doctors had diagnosed her with stage 4 lung cancer, that it was a rare strain of it and that it was terminal. Anna was the fittest, strongest, most outgoing woman I knew, she had panned my ass at the Iron Man triathlon we had both done, had won a military award for bravery, and just never stood still in life. She wouldn't let this beat her, it couldn't and wouldn't kill her. We made a plan to do anything and everything to help her beat this, researching holistic approaches towards cures, and a few months later I drove her to the Royal Marsden for her first chemo treatment. She created a list of challenges to complete in order to raise funds for various cancer charities. As crew gals, all of us rallied round her, as Anna still did not want the rest of our colleagues to know. Looking back now I wonder if she was like me and hated the idea of showing weakness or being a burden.

Throughout 2016 she continued with her treatment and was smashing it. She once admitted to me that the only thing she was scared of was losing her hair. Thankfully, she didn't and kept her bright blonde hair to match the bright sunny smile that we all knew and loved. She continued with her challenge list, and we were along for the ride, like it or lump it! We climbed Ben Nevis together in early 2017, she rode around London for twenty-four hours on Boris bikes, went to Barcelona for another Iron Man, and Anna parachuted out of a Chinook, thankfully on her own for this one. As 2017 went on she became sicker, she was selected for an immunotherapy trial and that seemed to work, and we all breathed a sigh of relief. Miracles can happen. She had been admitted to St Michael's Hospice but soon came out as her health began to improve. Then again in early summer Anna was readmitted to the hospice. Every time she went back in my heart sank a little more, wondering if this was the beginning of the end. But it was not. She improved again in late August and went to the Belgium Grand Prix to tick off another bucket-list moment.

Anna bounced in and out of the hospice more times than Tigger on speed. The joke with the nursing staff, who were amazing humans and became friends, was that Anna wanted to try out every room in there. We never wanted her to wake up in the middle of the night scared, so we all took turns to sleep by her side, either on the floor or folded up in a chair that was possibly the most uncomfortable piece of furniture known to man. We spent a lot of time with her over these months as her pain progressed. Seeing her wince in agony but knowing there was nothing we could do as her body wasted away was heartbreaking. We discussed trying to get our hands on cannabis oil to ease the pain for her but with us all still serving decided it wasn't a great idea as it was still illegal then. One afternoon when we were sitting with her, she said she wanted to throw a party to thank everyone for helping her with her challenges and fundraising. She had a clear idea of what she wanted in her mind. A 1940s themed hangar party at RAF Odiham, with everyone in costume and the ladies in 1940s dresses and victory rolls in their hair. She envisaged it all in great detail and wanted the night to end with a balloon drop from the roof. We all nodded away at one another, laughing at Anna's 'crazy ideas' but also knew we actually had to make this happen to give her something to live for. We started to put the vague plan together and then Anna took a massive downward turn. The doctors said she maybe had a week or two left. The planning went into turbo mode and was set to happen on Friday, 10 November 2017 in 18 Squadron's hangar. Everyone moved heaven and earth to help me plan it as they all knew and loved Anna so much. Nothing was too much trouble and ticket sales were going fast as everyone wanted to see her, and deep down they knew it may be the last time. She picked the dress she wanted to wear, despite being skin and bones now, and had her hair put in victory roles to practise how it would look.

The Friday, one week before the party, Anna's sister called us from the hospice. 'Come now', the words we dreaded to hear but knew were inevitable at some point. Skelfy and I raced down as we only lived round the corner and Claire arrived minutes later. The nurses were doing really well to hold it together but couldn't help but break down when they saw us in the corridor. Anna asked if she could go outside as she wanted to look at the sky. We got her into her wheelchair and pushed her through the open doors to the patio. She had been close to the edge so many times before but always bounced back. She stared up at the sky and a tear rolled down just one of her cheeks. Then she asked, 'Can I have some strawberry ice cream please?' 'Of course, hun,' as we took her back into her room. We left her sister there and hoped it was another of Anna's nearly-but-not-quite moments. Skelfy's phone rang just after 7 p.m. that evening. He didn't need to tell me, I instantly knew. He just held me as I sobbed then we poured a glass of champagne and toasted 'To Anna.'

A week later we threw one of the biggest hangar parties Odiham had ever seen. It went exponential as people pulled out all the stops to get there to celebrate Anna's wonderful life and her last wish. It had taken some engineering but at midnight as the last song came on, *Sky Full of Stars* by Coldplay, Martin, one of the event team, pulled the cord and hundreds of red, white, and blue balloons floated down on to everyone on the dance floor. I just stood from the sidelines and cried my heart out. This was the proudest non-Chinook related moment of my life and I hope I did her proud. Anna's death changed me forever. I have only one regret in my life and that is that it took Anna to fall sick before I started to appreciate our friendship. It made me realise that you only get one shot at life so you must fill it with love and happiness. We are all standing in a line waiting for our moment to leave this earth, but, unfortunately, we have no idea how many people are ahead of us in the queue, and you never know when your number will be called. After Anna passed away, I volunteered at St Michael's Hospice as a receptionist for a year. This place had given her the best care over the time she spent there. The nursing and support staff who work there really are a different breed and we built up quite a friendship with them over the months. I felt it was the least I could do to give back a little of my time and hopefully provide a smile for other people's loved ones coming through reception under the worst possible circumstances. I'd also become the chairwoman at my local British Legion that year, so the night after Anna's hangar party I had the honour to attend the Festival of Remembrance at the Royal Albert Hall. Watching this service on TV always makes me choke with tears but actually being there in the audience that night made it all the more poignant. As they sounded the Last Post and we stood in silence with the poppies falling from the ceiling all I could do was cry. Those twenty-four hours were filled with falling balloons, falling poppies and falling tears. The following week, we flew on the Chinook tasked to repatriate Anna to her home town up in Staffordshire where the funeral would be held a week later. I mentioned earlier how hard I found ramp ceremonies at Bastion but nothing will ever compare to how hard I found this ceremony. The whole of RAF Odiham and local friends and families who knew Anna formed up on the aircraft dispersal as six of her best crewmen mates carried her in a Union flag-draped coffin on to the aircraft at sunrise. The girls and I then climbed on board to escort her up to Stafford where her parents were waiting. I was in pieces and was very unsure how this flight would leave me emotionally in the long run, but as soon as we were on board and in our familiar environment I relaxed. As the crew put the restraint strops carefully over the coffin, they said 'Property of the RAF' along them in black writing. How apt I thought and smiled. Her funeral was massive and the Chinook force did her proud with a missing man flypast over the top where one aircraft breaks off to the side. We had *Champagne Supernova* played, which was her favourite song and there wasn't a dry eye in the house. After the funeral, we went with the family to the crematorium; all of Staffordshire's police force had lined the route and saluted the hearse as it went past. At the end of the crematorium service, I didn't think I could take any more emotional wrecking balls and was dreading what she had picked for her last song ... then S Club 7 *Reach for the Stars* came on and we just all burst out laughing as she disappeared behind the curtain. That was Anna, making people smile right to the end.

Now I hate the idea of ending a chapter telling you about our amazing Anna on a sad note as that's just not her. She was full of joy and laughter so I shall leave you with this story.

When I stayed over at the hospice, I never managed to get any sleep so was always starving by morning. Anna's brekkie with a tray full of toast would arrive, and she would smother it in Marmite. I hated Marmite but I must admit it looked and smelled so good! She always offered me some, but I couldn't steal my sick friend's brekkie could I, so off I went to work dreaming of Marmite on toast. She was obsessed with it and took a little jar everywhere even to Belgium for the Grand Prix excursion. One night, Claire was round at our house and we were having a few drinks and chatting about Anna. I said to Claire that maybe it was time we revisited the cannabis oil idea we had previously poo poo'ed, as Anna was now in so much pain. Claire just laughed and went, 'Mate, what do you think her sister puts in the Marmite?' Thank God I never let Anna feed me any before work. What a legend, what a gal. Anna Irwin, you made the days count. I hope you are enjoying the *Champagne Supernova* up there, a dreamer dreams, she never dies, wipe that tear away now from your eye …

Chapter 14

The Domino Effect

Looking back, Anna's death was the first in a series of dominoes that began to topple in my life. The day after her funeral I ended up in A and E, and not with a hangover surprisingly but kidney stones. I have had kidney stones three times throughout my career. I have a relatively high pain threshold and am known for it. I once ran 8 miles with a fractured pelvis; I did my Iron Man with a broken foot and my previous kidney stone attacks didn't require me being admitted to hospital. I was informed that the main catalyst for them is bottled water, dusty environments, and dehydration – that explains why a few of my crewman mates had suffered the same ailment. They are the most excruciatingly painful thing I have ever experienced and I woke up the morning after Anna's funeral and Skelfy just knew instantly to take me straight to A and E, he too was aware of my stupidly high pain threshold and knew something really bad was happening. We raced down the country from Stafford in his campervan, nearly diverting into Oxford hospital before making it back to Basingstoke A and E where he had to carry me into the waiting area. The pain had been building in my side for around six days but, as I said earlier, it's amazing what your mind can block out when it needs to. I remained in hospital for a few days and then came home to pack my bags to head to my rehabilitation course at Headley Court in my last effort to resolve my neck pain. Ten days prior to all this, I had developed a pain in my groin while running at the gym one evening. Again, amid all the stress in life, this was my coping mechanism and one that was much needed with everything that had happened with Anna.

I mentioned this on arrival to the physio team at Headley Court and they sent me for an MRI straight away after reading my abundant history of stress fractures in my ever-growing file of medical notes. The MRI showed I had fractured my pelvis AGAIN, for the second time in my life! In a nutshell, during the week running up to Anna's funeral I had been carrying a kidney stone and walking around with a broken pelvis, but my body held itself together somehow until what was needed to be done was over. Almost like a repeat performance of my neck in the Falklands.

A few months later, in January 2018, I had my official medical board to decide my future in the RAF. I put on my number one best blues, for what I expected to be the last time and travelled up to RAF Henlow. There I would face a review of my medical notes and a decision from a Group Captain (senior RAF officer) whether the RAF would retain me in service or discharge me. I had resigned myself to the fact that I was leaving and as the Group Captain sat opposite me, he clasped his hands together and informed me that he would be downgrading my medical category but keeping me in the service. I was speechless. For the first time in my life, absolutely speechless. My head was swimming, and I honestly couldn't process his words. My new medical category read along the lines of: unfit deployment both UK and overseas, no weapon handling, no training exercises, no guard duty, no fitness test, basically no life. He had inadvertently handcuffed me to a desk to see out my career and about the only thing I was fit for was emptying the blooming bins. I left feeling angry. Angry that despite being a broken shell and having the one job I had given my life to stripped away from me they weren't willing to let me go and find a new career path as a civilian. I got back to Odiham to seek the advice of our senior medical officer straight away. She was wonderful and having seen the stresses on me over the previous twelve months knew just how fragile I was. She advised me that I could challenge the decision if I wished and argue my case for a medical discharge, citing mental health degradation if I did stay behind a desk. I simply could not remain in the RAF to sit in an office wearing blues all day, I knew it would destroy me mentally. A few mates said you have got the 'Carlsberg' of med cats and they are paying you to do nothing, just take it, but I couldn't face myself in the mirror every day and not feel that sense of pride I had in being a crewman. I took her advice and challenged the board's decision a week later. This time I was finally granted a medical discharge and a different form of freedom, one to start my life over again.

It was a bittersweet feeling knowing that I was leaving. Although it had ultimately been my choice, I would have given anything to stay in and continue to fly. That is what I joined the RAF to do and what my passion was. It also coincided with me being written up for a Queen's Commendation for services to the Chinook force. A lovely surprise when I was mentioned on the Queen's Birthday Honours list and a wonderful acknowledgement of my career, a fitting final farewell no less. Later I was also informed that I had been written up for my next promotion to the rank of Master Aircrewman which would have made me the first Chinook Aircrew 'mistress' as I joked. But this was still not enough to tie me to a desk for my life. The rank for me was never important, it was doing the job that meant everything to me. I had a year of resettlement courses to learn how to transition into civilian life and most of 2018 was spent at home as I was not officially 'allowed' to be in work due to insurance reasons. My last official day in service was 11 January 2019, and two months later I received my commendation, awarded in the officers' mess by Group Captain Lee Turner, who was the station commander at the time and had, by then, become a longstanding and valued friend. I arrived home to find my Veterans' pin badge and Veterans' ID card had been delivered in the post. I poured a glass of champagne and toasted with Skelfy to the end of an era and being a 'Veteran' at just 37. Skelfy had also come to the natural end of his 22-year career in the army around the same time, so he too was spending a lot of time at home kicking his heels. Now ideally this would have been the perfect time to disappear off around the world travelling or put our bikes on the campervan and head off on a carefree adventure, but we couldn't. I had lots of little courses and appointments to attend, and Skelfy was in the early throes of setting up his own business so was tied to his laptop most days and getting last-minute jobs coming in sporadically. We started to argue a lot more. Looking back now I think we were both struggling within ourselves in our lack of purpose and structure. We were both indoctrinated and had spent our entire adult lives in the military and not just that but doing very significant and dangerous jobs in the forces. Life for both of us now seemed very 'vanilla'. We felt like a pair of 'has-beens'. It's bad enough saying I used to be in the 'military' as you sound like one of those old vets who can't let it go but imagine saying 'I used to be in the SAS'; you instantly just sound like a wannabe. Sadly, we were both sinking at the same time, so it was hard to try and rescue one another from drowning, and we were both also in complete denial, and searching to find our new identities now we were out of the military. Looking back with hindsight we both had lots of unresolved traumatic experiences in our heads that we had packaged up and locked in the depths of its chambers. This constant exposure to trauma and danger over the years manifested with both of our brains being in a constant fight response mode. In turn this led to us triggering one another all the time and feeling as if we were constantly walking on eggshells around each other, trying not to kick off the next row. Neither of us were wrong in that observation of feeling on tenterhooks as it was in fact the truth for us both. That's what I have learnt with age: every story has two truths, two perceptions and views or opinions on what or who is correct. These come from within a person and are built on their beliefs and feelings, therefore no one can ever be truly wrong in an emotionally charged argument as it's 'their truth' and what they are perceiving. Because we buried our heads in the sand and tried the classic 'man up' we refused to address our own issues and began blaming one another for everything that went wrong. We stopped being on the same team, which had always been our strength. We were almost like Mr and Mrs Smith from the film, loads of riotous fights but when we were both fighting the same enemy, we were OK, for a while at least. It's a shame we didn't realise at any point when arguing, as our marriage crumbled, that we were now fighting the same invisible enemy. Over the years we'd had many ups and downs and plenty of time in counselling. We had also spent time apart both forced through work and voluntarily to gain some space and perspective. Skelfy said Anna's death had changed me and he was right. It hadn't changed me as a person, but it had changed my outlook on life. I realised life was too short to be this unhappy. In March 2019, I moved out for a trial separation and for self-preservation. A choice that I didn't take lightly, and I knew Skelfy didn't want. Within twenty-four hours I felt as though a black cloud had been lifted. Skelfy had been the love of my life since the very first day I met him. When we were good, we were really good, but when we were bad, we were awful. We had become toxic for one another and pulling in opposite directions. It was time to finally make the next toughest decision and again, one I knew deep in my heart was the right one, despite the heartbreak it would involve. I asked for a divorce.

So, it had been a pretty rubbish eighteen months all up I can honestly say. Anna dying followed by a medical discharge from the job I loved and lived for, followed by the end of a fairy-tale marriage, and saying goodbye to the only man I had ever loved and a family that had taken me under its wing. But my overwhelming emotion at that time was relief. Relief to be set free from the RAF and the sentence of a desk job for life and to break free from a marriage that had become a constant battleground. I had started a new job with an amazing charity called Aerobility who taught disabled people how to fly and I loved it. Aerobility flies a little fleet of adapted airplanes to allow anyone with any disability how to fly. They are based out of Blackbushe Airport, only fifteen minutes down the road from Odiham – yet I had never heard of them. From the first minute I visited, having been invited down by another army friend to see what they do, I was bowled over by what I saw and the difference they were making to people's lives. Finally, I had purpose again and my role was to co-ordinate the wounded injured soldiers' (WIS) flying scholarships. It was amazing to see some of the amputees, who our Chinooks had scooped up off the battlefield years before, find their way into the skies and achieve PPLs. The banter was just like being back on the squadron and I was so content. A few months later I was offered a job working back at Odiham in the simulator. I wasn't sure if it was really my thing as I hate technical stuff and computers, but all the people I had worked with over the years were there as staff and I thought it would be just like being back in the RAF with all my mates. I handed my notice in at Aerobility with such a heavy heart and cried my eyes out the afternoon I left, before heading to begin this 'too good to be true' job back at Odiham, this time dressed as a civilian.

Within a few weeks I knew I had made the biggest mistake of my life. It was nothing like I expected. Firstly, and most importantly, my new uniform of a black polo shirt and cargo pants made me look like a grade A lesbian again. Let's not revisit that, shall we? I basically spent each day in a large soulless building from 0800 to 1700 and when the crews arrived, they briefed their training sortie before crewing into the SIM, flying it then leaving. It wasn't at all like being on the squadron and although it was a virtual reality simulator worth millions of pounds it had so many technical issues in the early days of set up that it was always breaking. It soon dawned on me that I was basically just going to press buttons on a massive computer screen for the rest of my life. It could not have been a worse fit for me in any way. The company was amazing and really looked after me, especially as they knew that I was going through, what was fast becoming, a messy divorce, but my boss was a friend of Skelfy and it made life miserable working with him daily. I handed my notice in five months later. I was walking away from the best-paid job I had ever had and one most people would kill for, to go to nothing, no plan

B. But I knew I could not stay. My boss said 'You are either really brave or really stupid.' I hoped it was the former, but I was scared at the same time. The thing I did have though was faith, and as long as you have faith you are allowed to be scared as you know it will turn out OK in the end. Faith had helped me many times before and I trusted my judgement.

That November in 2019 my divorce came through. My emotions by this time had gone from relief to anger as Skelfy had not made my life easy over the previous few months but I guess he was trying to deal with it in his own way. That same month, I attended the Aviators' Ball which Aerobility use as their main fundraising event. It's a huge black-tie dinner held at Sofitel Heathrow every year and I had secured my tickets much earlier, back in April when I had briefly worked for them. It instantly felt as though I was amongst friends again when I walked into the lobby. Later that night I was chatting to Mike the CEO and founder of Aerobility and my boss at the charity who had been extremely understanding when I left after such a short period of time with them. He asked how I was, and said he was sorry to hear about Skelfy and me. He followed up in asking how the new job at the simulator was. I was honest and told him that I had hated it and really regretted leaving Aerobility. I knew my old job was already taken but I just needed Mike to know how much I regretted leaving them. He said, 'Call me on Monday, I have an idea.' The following week after chatting to Mike, a new position as a Project Manager opened up for me back at Aerobility, or the 'dream factory' as I lovingly call it. Very quickly, Aerobility had become almost family to me, they were the new crewmen in my life. They always had my back and looked after me. I didn't know back then how much I would come to rely on them the following year.

All in all, by January 2020, despite so many dominoes tumbling over I felt that life was finally on the up. I had a great job again, one with mission and purpose for a charity which made a difference in the world. I would routinely go home on a Friday with face ache from laughing so hard in the office with my colleagues, Marcus, Harvey, Neil and Stuart. I had briefly dated a lovely guy who gave me my confidence back and helped me find my smile again. And I was smashing my running out of the park with personal bests almost weekly. Then in March 2020 a little thing called Covid arrived on UK shores and all our worlds changed FOREVER. My colleague Chad and I watched it unfold from news updates on our laptops throughout February. As it reached UK soils, we were all sent to work from home as our flyers and supporters were all in the high-risk group. A week later, Boris Johnson locked the UK down. When we entered lockdown, I lived alone in my old flat that I had bought back in 2007 off plan. I had been away in Afghanistan the year I bought it and when it was completed, my mate Burnsy moved in for me as I had given him power of attorney. I remember arriving back from Helmand to see it. I had landed from a MERT shout and my boss at the time met me at the ramp and said, 'Liz, pack your bags you're going home tonight.' I instantly thought, yikes what have I done, why am I being sent home? But it turned out that he had the option of getting two people out a few days early on the TriStar back to RAF Brize Norton. He decided that Birty, whose wife had just had a baby, and me, having just bought my first flat were the most deserved. Off I went to pack my kit up from my little bedspace and within twelve hours was standing in my brand-new apartment in Basingstoke, having been handed the keys by the Squadron Ops staff. I had a meltdown. A full-on meltdown. All I could focus on was that I had no curtains. I didn't, but I also had no sofa, TV, fridge, or anything in terms of furnishings but it was the lack of curtains that caused the emotional breakdown. After a teary phone call to my mum, I levelled up, but it highlighted to me how dangerous it can be to come back from theatre without some form of decompression to get you back to normal thinking. Years later, the armed forces also realised this and factored a few days decompression into the journey back from Op Herrick for all troops. This was met with much contempt at the time as most of us just wanted to get home to our loved ones, not spend two days in Cyprus having enforced fun and a chat from the padre. But this decompression was essential, it's just a shame the heads of sheds didn't realise it sooner and for many it came too late in the Herrick campaign.

I had finally moved back into Hollies Court after six months, having rented another tiny apartment while waiting for the divorce to come through. It was like a time warp being back in it all these years later and I only intended to stay there for a few months while selling it to buy a new place and have a completely fresh start in life. However, this was not to be, and I spent the whole of this first lockdown on my own, in my crummy old flat, just me and my four walls, no pets or even plants to look after. What had been my shelter and my place to retreat to had now become my prison. I had no garden and no plus-one bubble as they were not sanctioned by then. Oh, but I did have company most nights, my thoughts. They would invade my brain the second my head hit the pillow and would tumble around like a marble in a noisy washing machine all night. I began to suffer from insomnia. I initially helped on a project set up by my good friend Neil from Aerobility called Print for Victory. I helped co-ordinate a volunteer army of home-based 3D printer enthusiasts to manufacture visor shields for care homes and small GP practices. It was all-consuming, but it gave me a reason to get up every morning. Each day we would get more and more calls from those small groups of forgotten front-line workers. Hearing their heartache as they begged for help down the telephone and their gratitude and tears of thanks as they received them made it all worth it, but I was living on cornflakes. I was so busy I barely left the house, even for a quick run each day which Boris had permitted us to do. During these frantic weeks, I formed a new routine of living on convenience food and barely leaving the house to get any sunlight or exercise. But after two weeks giving our heart and souls to help people in need, government legislation kicked in and in the space of twenty-four hours Print for Victory, and many other home-turf helpers were shut down, without any acknowledgement or thanks for what they had achieved. My daily purpose and routine had now gone, but I unfortunately found myself with a new routine of poor nutrition and lack of exercise and no purpose whatsoever, in fact no real reason to get out of bed each day. My coping mechanism over the years had always been keeping busy and suddenly that was not an option with the endless days of lockdown. I didn't want to do DIY as I intended to move soon, I had no garden to tend to and I didn't want to waste money shopping, so all I did was watch Netflix and eat. I spent longer and longer periods of time in the house without leaving it to get fresh air. I used to stare at the front door daily and will myself to go out but just couldn't. My bike and trainers were stacked in the hallway, almost taunting me to touch them. But every time I went near them with intentions of doing some exercise, my brain let me down and I recoiled in self-defeat retreating to the safety of the sofa, or bed. Things began to unravel as the weeks of lockdown turned to months with no end in sight. I found myself getting up in the middle of the night and hunting desperately for my logbook then beginning to google the soldiers that had lost their lives on Op Herrick and seeing which ones I had picked up during my time on MERT. My diet spiralled out of control bingeing on sugary foods to try and help lift my mood on the dark days, and the more I ate the less I wanted to run or even walk. I was hitting self-destruct in spectacular fashion, as many Veterans tend to do. Self-sabotage is a well-known symptom that comes with PTSD and depression; we don't just let the wheels come off, we blow the whole damn truck up. I knew I was heading in a very bad direction and that I was struggling badly, but did I tell anyone how I was feeling? Don't be ridiculous, little Liz McC is the happiest, smiley, most motivated, healthy girl we know. Look at all her amazing photos on Facebook of how great her life is. I was the master of disguise. No one had any idea how much I was falling apart and how quickly it was gathering pace. Just the same as all those years as a crewman, I didn't want to be a burden.

Chapter 15

Time to End a Life

I will write this chapter exactly as it happened, not because it's cathartic but because I hope my experiences may help others. Lockdown had lasted much longer than we all expected. By June, my little brother Stewart, thankfully, came to stay with me for work and it was just so fab having him around each night. We had such a laugh and really reconnected as brother and sister after years of only catching up at Christmas back at the family home in Newtownards. He's a little legend and one of the funniest and most cheerful people in the world and he rescued me from the depths of loneliness and despair I was feeling at the time. I still had my dark moments but him arriving home each night was the highlight of my otherwise dull day. He had no idea at the time of the suffering that was going on within my brain and I hid it all so well, mostly as when he was around, life was bright. He stayed at mine until the end of July and then had to move on for work. I missed him instantly and had just my thoughts for company again. August arrived and so did the hottest heatwave on record in the UK. I was already struggling to sleep, and this just compounded the problem. I would lie awake all night with the windows wide open, listening to Chinooks fly past on night training, and revisiting the past over and over, while not sleeping. Another thing that, looking back now, may have added to my spiralling out of control was that my mate Claire who was still flying on Chinooks had a wire strike that week. Thankfully, all the crew were fine and landed safely but seeing the pictures in the national press instantly took me back to the day of my wire strike over thirteen years earlier at Kajaki, and the first time I thought I might die. The smell of burning electricity was instantly back in my nostrils.

On Saturday, 8 August, my best mate Sue and I decided it was time to hit the town and make the most of lockdown recently being lifted and the spell of good weather. We had a fab night out in our local town having dinner, drinking Prosecco, and dancing the night away! So much so that I didn't get home until about 0300 which was barely unheard of for me these days. The following morning, I dragged myself out of bed as I was going to Blenheim Palace with a few of the crew gals and their kids. I had never been to Blenheim before, and it was a blissful day despite my hangover. Playing in the gardens with the kids, taking trips on a little train and eating ice creams in the sunshine. I got home that Sunday evening and my brother swung in for a brew before he headed off to his new site slightly further south. I sat down and thought how lucky I was to have come through lockdown and have such great mates and family. My Facebook posts reflected just that. Pictures of myself and Sue in our little dresses and then the girls and I on the train with the munchkins, all smiles. That night though I knew I had to try and get some proper sleep, having not slept properly for five days now. I had been prescribed a drug called amitriptyline back in 2018 for headaches I was getting, which the doctors suspected were connected to my neck injury. Amitriptyline is a nerve blocker, so great for these types of issues and many Veterans take it for ghost pains and nerve damage. It also happens to be the most amazing sleeping tablet and is well known for it and one of the most prescribed drugs by the NHS. I had stopped taking it routinely back in late 2019 as I hate being on painkillers – it has never been my thing despite my frequent injuries. But I had taken one of these tablets the odd night before a big day at work to help me sleep with no issues whatsoever. So that Sunday night, I took one of my trusty amitriptyline and drifted straight off to the land of nod. Bliss.

I woke feeling refreshed on the Monday morning and realised that I only had one pack of the drug left having used it sporadically over the previous years. I reordered it with the pharmacy online that morning as it was on a repeat prescription. Monday went on as normal, and I took another that evening as it was still around 25 degrees at night when I was trying to sleep. On the Tuesday evening, I went for a lovely long walk and met my bestie Sue at the pub halfway between her house and mine. We had a soda water each as we were both back on a health kick after the calorie fest from the previous Saturday night. Off I went back home, lovely salad for dinner and another tablet.

I woke up on the Wednesday morning to another bright sunny day. But my mood had significantly shifted and all I can say is that I felt as though I had been body snatched by the grim reaper. I did not feel as if I was in control of my brain; it was as if I was having an out of body experience. I decided that today was going to be my last day on earth and it was the most normal and logical decision I had ever made. I logged on to my 10 a.m. Zoom call with Aerobility and chatted away as normal, or so I thought. After that something triggered inside, and I knew I should try and reach out to get professional help. Firstly, I emailed my GP surgery explaining that I had woken up suicidal and really needed help. I got a reply from the pharmacy, stating I had emailed them by mistake and to contact the surgery to resolve my 'issue', so I rang the practice. Initially, the receptionist said they were making emergency appointments only and a doctor would call me back later that week. I burst into tears and said I really think I need to speak to someone today. The receptionist instantly picked up on my desperation and said she would get someone to call me that afternoon. He rang just after lunch. I explained through my tears that I had woken up with suicidal thoughts and that I was really worried as this was so unlike me and so out of character.

He asked if I lived alone, which I did now my brother had moved out. I explained that I only lived about thirty seconds walk from the surgery which I could almost see from my apartment. After much, 'Yes, I understand, yes it sounds like you're depressed etc.,' he prescribed me a drug called sertraline, an anti-depressant, and said it would be ready to collect that afternoon. He recommended I took it that afternoon but warned me it would make me feel worse before I felt better. At no point did he say, 'Would you like to come in and speak to someone face to face?' At no point did he ask what other medication I was on. And critically, he did not check on my notes to see that I had been prescribed amitriptyline previously and had reordered it less than forty-eight hours before. Most importantly on hanging up the call, he never asked again, whether or not I was still considering killing myself, which I was. It turns out that amitriptyline is also an anti-depressant and can hijack your mood. I only know this now having done some research on it. Much like alcohol, drinking when you're down can make you further depressed or drinking when you're happy elevates your mood. I had never been told this before and had never experienced this as a side-effect either when taking the drug. If the doctor had asked that vital question 'What medication are you currently taking' when we spoke, or indeed got me to go to the surgery the next sequence of events may not have happened.

They say when you are drowning there is a distinctive point where your body accepts what is happening and stops fighting and relaxes. This was that moment for me that day. I accepted my fate on hanging up that call that I would be dying that evening and that this was my final day to have to battle and honestly it felt as if a huge weight had been lifted off my shoulders rather weirdly. If I was on a water slide, I had collected my donut ring and wasn't scared anymore to try the slide. I was in position about to be pushed into the tunnel. The GP had given me that little shove and I was now merrily on my way, no way back. Here is how the rest of Wednesday, 12 August 2020 went:

14.00   I hung up the phone to the doctor, still in tears, and in my head decided that no one cared if I lived or died. In desperation, I had attempted to reach out for help but he hadn't listened.

14.00–15.00   I spent the afternoon googling how much amitriptyline it would take to kill me for my body weight. I went on suicide websites to read stories from survivors who had tried it. There is a worrying amount of advice on the internet on how to kill yourself it seems. Mostly from survivors who have made an attempt and failed but are now passing on their knowledge to others who are planning their death. I can't believe these websites even exist looking back and is something that needs addressing by the internet police urgently. From these stories on the various forums, I was able to calculate how many amitriptyline I would need to do some damage and how many I would need to kill myself outright with no chance of recovery. I knew that with the remaining fifteen I had along with the dose of eighty that I was waiting to pick up I would have ninety-five in total. This, I calculated would put me right in the bracket of 50/50 die or survive depending on several things including my body's strength, food that I had in my tummy and how quickly I was found, if at all, of course. I also knew that I had a 'bonus' prescription of sertraline now coming my way so if I wanted to, I could do the job outright. I had a notepad and pen while working all this out and wrote down all my calculations. My brother found these a

146

few days later when I was still in hospital and assumed it was the medic's handwriting calculating what I had taken. I didn't have the heart to tell him that it was my premeditated maths calculations. No other method of extinction crossed my mind. I didn't think to hang myself, jump off a bridge in front of a train or drink a bottle of bleach. All of which could have been possible. I say this now as I often wonder if we are predisposed in some way to know how we would like to die? All I wanted to do was go to sleep forever and not feel any pain; maybe I'm too much of a scaredy-cat to actually want to hurt myself while dying (rather hilariously). I've always thought suicide is a cowardly thing to do, but when you are in that place, which I hope you never are, you will realise that your brain sees no other option. All of this seemed at the time the most normal thing in the world. I was on a one-way mission. I was in the tunnel, and nothing could stop me from success at this point. I was on my way down the slide, gathering momentum.

15.30   Sue texted to see how I was. She had known I was having good and bad days over lockdown and checked in with me every afternoon to make sure I was fine. I replied that things were good, I was feeling positive and that I had a plan. (Sue said looking back now she was gutted she didn't pick up on that sentence at the time, but, remember, I was all smiles and the master of disguise.)

16.00   I walked over to collect my now-lethal dose of drugs. The lady in the pharmacy handed me two separate white paper bags, one containing my amitriptyline and one with my sertraline. Even at this point, despite receiving my email by mistake earlier that day with my plea for help, no one noted my call for help and stepped in at this vital point. The irony was I had to pay for my prescriptions, and I remember getting my card out to pay the sum total of £13 for the privilege of killing myself. I was almost laughing to myself by now, I was so emotionally detached. But sadly, no one in the pharmacy picked up on what they had just handed over to me in each of these bags.

16.20   The Wednesday night posh fish and chip van that parked up at our community centre was just opening his shutters as I walked the thirty seconds back to my apartment. I never eat fish and chips, and pre-Covid I had always had the cleanest diet, but I thought to myself 'Fuck it, if I'm going to have a last dinner I may as well have chips.' I walked over and looked up at the jolly man with his green striped apron. I asked if he was open yet and he said, 'Depends on what you want, dear.' I replied, 'Just some chips please.' He said, 'Well I've just put some on for my son's dinner,' and nodded at a young lad sitting on the worktop, 'You can have his and I'll do him some more,' laughing at his now hungry-looking lad and smiling. He asked if I wanted salt and vinegar to which I mindlessly said 'No', then instantly said 'I mean yes.' He laughed again and said, 'It's not a difficult question, love.' It was the nicest conversation I'd had that day so far. Off I went with my drugs and chips, happy as Larry.

17.00   I had finished my chips, so set to writing my suicide note. This mentioned my parents and brothers obviously, along with my sisters-in-law and my two little twin nieces, the love of my life. I also apologised to Sue and my friend Andy Davidson who had both looked out for me so much throughout lockdown. As I wrote it, I thought about them all. I had always thought suicide was the most selfish act a person could do, yet here I was completely void of emotion, not a tear in sight, writing my letter. I thought about not seeing my nieces grow up. Oh well. I thought of not seeing my little brother get married in October as was planned. Oh well. I thought about Anna and how she had her life taken away from her and here I was giving mine up. Oh well. I added to the bottom of the note what songs I wanted played at my funeral ... more of that in a minute. I simply could not connect any emotion to my thoughts and feelings.

18.00   I fed my little bearded dragon, Rupert, with loads of salad leaves and crickets. I've always had bearded dragons as pets, my first was called Dave after Grohly and my second was Bernard who had stayed with Skelfy when we separated. Rupert had been my little sidekick during lockdown, and I was sad to say goodbye to him as I loaded his tank with enough food to survive a few days until someone could find him and look after him. But I was not the emotional wreck I should have been when looking at his little face. My heart by now was cold and empty.

19.00   I texted my little brother to say have a fab weekend as he was flying back up to Scotland for his birthday. I signed off with 'Love ya'. Which wasn't that unusual. I then texted my mum to say have a lovely weekend in Donegal and that I loved her. This was unusual as I'm rubbish at telling her I love her. She also says looking back now she should have suspected something, but again I had all the smoke and mirrors in place.

20.00   Cleaned the house from top to bottom, emptied the fridge and took out the trash.

22.00   Had a shower, did my hair and make-up, and put on a lovely maxi dress.

23.00   I placed my suicide note in an envelope and put it on my dining room table, ironically, I don't recall writing a name on it. Just a white envelope, sitting alone on the wooden table.

23.30   Left the door on the latch and unlocked my phone. Again, I had decided that if I was putting myself in the hands of fate, I would give fate a fighting chance. This interests me now looking back as I feel that somewhere inside me, I didn't really want to die. But at the time I did. I 100 per cent intended to go sleep and never wake up.

23.40   I sat down on my bed with my pile of drugs beside me and a pint glass of water, the little bedside light on.

23.45   Texted both Sue my bestie and Andy D a message thanking them for all their love and support during lockdown.

23.50   Posted my two favourite pictures of myself on my Instagram and Facebook page in the hope that they may be used at my funeral. (Yes, this is where my mind was at.) Along with the song *In the Arms of the Angels* which I had noted in my suicide letter that I wanted at my funeral, along with *Gimme Shelter* by the Rolling Stones and *Sound of Silence* by Disturbed (at least I still had pretty good music taste to the end).

00.00   I very calmly began to swallow the first of the ninety-five amitriptyline one at time. I wasn't sick and I seem to remember it taking less than five minutes all up to finish them all. Thankfully, all this was done without a drop of alcohol involved. Although I like a social drink, I have never turned to alcohol to solve my problems, and never drink alone. A crucial habit that may have saved my life.

I do not remember anything else from that night with any amount of clarity. But I can tell you that I didn't cry once, even when I had taken them all. And I at no point regretted anything with each little white pill I swallowed, even when I knew I was past the point of no return and into the 50/50 survive or die bracket. I was emotionless. Void of any feeling. Done. Worn out. Drained. Mentally Exhausted. I just wanted to go to sleep forever.

I am not sure if my brain imagined this or it actually happened, but I think at one point I heard someone on my phone saying, 'stay awake, do NOT go to sleep.'

But I remember feeling blissfully relaxed and free as I ignored those words and closed my eyes for the last time, my brain finally at peace.

Chapter 16

Just Breathe

'She's awake' ... the words I hear as my eyes bang open.

I had no idea where I was or what was happening, there were faces staring down at me in masks and saying 'Elizabeth' over and over. There were noises beeping loudly and I couldn't move. I had a tube down my throat and started to panic as I tried to breathe, it felt as though I was drowning. The irony is that suddenly the prospect of death scared me so much. I tried to grab at this tube and pull at it. Then I went back to sleep. I woke up again and the faces were there once more but talking to me this time and explaining that I had to relax, and I was OK. This was the scariest moment of my entire life. I lay there still feeling as if I was drowning in fluid. Trying to swallow but unable to; entirely helpless. My mantra of just breathe was not working as I had no control over it and was sporadically choking. I could feel tears rolling down my cheeks as I felt trapped, no breath, no movement, no voice. My leaking eyes were panicked and wide open, looking at these people and almost trying to beg them with the windows to my soul to save me as I couldn't cry out the words 'HELP ME.'

What I did not grasp at this moment was that they had. This was me coming out the other side of a forty-hour coma on life support. I stared at the clock on the wall across from the bed I now lay in and the hands were at 6.30. I assumed it was 0630 on the Thursday morning, but it was indeed now Friday, I was informed. All I could feel was this tube and all I could see was that clock. The faces arrived again and explained that they were going to take the tube out of my throat, and they would have to get me to gag it up. This event surpassed the feeling of drowning as the new worst experience I'd ever been through. I have very little medical knowledge which was probably a good thing. They placed something down my throat, and I instantly gagged, the tube moved, I panicked even more, there were beepers going off. They did it again and it moved some more. I panicked further thinking it was all going wrong, then with the final gag they pulled this thing that I thought was killing me out of my throat. It was obviously the intubation tube that had in fact been keeping me alive.

I now was able to try and speak but I had no voice. I looked down and both my arms had tubes in them and were black and blue from my hands to my elbows with deep bruising. I could still feel a tube in my nose. I just lay there with big heavy tears now slowly tumbling down my cheeks, not because I had a concept of what had happened but because I did not. I had no idea what state my body was in or how I had got there. The doctor started to explain that I was OK and was in HDU in Basingstoke Hospital. He said I had been brought in by an ambulance crew and been put on life support in the early hours of Thursday morning. I still couldn't speak to ask him any questions, so I just lay there like a vegetable, looking at him through my glassy eyes. He informed me that they were concerned about my heart and they were monitoring it closely but otherwise I was fine. He told me that they had managed to get hold of my mum and tell her I was in the hospital and would get her on the phone for me as soon as I felt able. It dawned on me what had happened. How could I speak to my mum, what could I say? 'I'm sorry I tried to kill myself.' What must she be going through? No, what had I put her through?

As the morning went on, I tried to piece things together from the limited information I had, i.e. brought in by ambulance. I recall everything up until sitting on the bed and taking the pills but still no idea how an ambulance crew had found me. It is a horrible feeling having a section of time erased from your memory. We've all had those nights when we have drunk too much and wake up the next morning with the dreaded fear of 'What did I do?' but this was different. This was 'How did I survive?' I tried to speak, but my voice was barely there. Just a hoarse quiet whimper. My throat was still damaged from the tube. A few hours later, they removed the smaller tube from my nose that led to my stomach, another highlight to add to the ongoing trauma. The doctor asked again if I would like to speak to my mum on the phone. I still said no. He nodded with understanding and said that he would give her an update on my behalf. I spent that morning hallucinating while just lying there, having checks carried out on me every twenty minutes. I was convinced there was a nurse standing by the wall on my right-hand side. I couldn't see her properly, just her outline and she never moved, just stayed there watching me. It turns out this nurse was the container for the blue medical roll that was mounted to the wall by my bed. I also watched as the curly leads on the ECG machine a few feet from the end of my bed spiralled up and down, getting shorter then longer as they twirled. After the drugs began to wear off, I realised their little dance was all in my head. I've never ever done drugs in my life, never even smoked. Yes, I enjoy a drink but that's it, always has been. I can only guess that this is what it must feel like to be on some form of hallucinogenic pills and an experience I would not like to repeat.

A few hours later, the nurse came over to tell me that my little brother Stewart was here at the hospital and was I ready to see him. Oh my God, Stewart. How must he be feeling, I'd totally ruined his birthday was my first thought. I nodded to the nurse who smiled and went to fetch him. Thankfully, with the breathing and nose tubes now gone I hoped I didn't look too scary for him to see. As he walked round the curtain my heart shattered seeing his face. He was in pieces. This is the reality of suicide. Staring at his face and seeing all his unanswered questions in his eyes made me realise what gets left behind when someone takes their own life. When you have an accident and you survive, people arrive at your bedside with a face of relief that you are OK. Stewart clearly was, but his expression wasn't relief, it was just pure heartbreak and questioning sadness. We hugged and just cried, with him repeating, 'Why didn't you tell me? Why didn't you say something?' We sat together as I went through what had happened and told him how I needed him to know he couldn't have done anything to change what I did, and that he had done nothing wrong. In fact, he had done quite the opposite. He had kept me going for much longer that summer than I would have managed without him. A few minutes later his fiancée, Kirsty, came to join us as she had wanted to give us some time alone so had waited downstairs. I sat there with them both, trying to piece together what had happened and fill in some blanks.

Stewart had flown home that Thursday, back to Glasgow. When he stepped off the plane, he turned his phone on and it was my mum telling him, 'Elizabeth has taken an overdose and is on life support in HDU.' He got to his house, got in the car with Kirsty and started to drive south. I had been taken into the hospital by ambulance in the early hours of Thursday, but they hadn't been able to get hold of my parents until late Thursday afternoon. Mum and Dad had been away at their holiday home in Donegal but the hospital had been trying the landline for our family home back in Northern Ireland that was registered on my medical notes. Probably a good thing, looking back, as my mum would have crumbled. She makes worrying a national sport and if she had been told earlier when I was still critical, she would have jumped on a plane to fly over, which would have been awful for both her and me. When they did get finally get hold of her, I was still on life support and although the doctor said they still didn't know if I would make it or not, I stood a good chance. She and my dad made their way back across the border while looking at flights etc., but thankfully my brothers took control and said they would come to my side first.

Despite all this information, I still had no idea how an ambulance had found me, nor indeed how the hospital had finally got hold of my mum on her mobile number. Stewart said the name 'Sue?' He told me she had spoken to Mum at some point. None of my family have ever met Sue so they didn't really know how important a part of my life she was. 'Sue?' I questioned? 'Did she find me that night?' I had so many questions going through my head. I didn't have my phone; my only personal effects at the hospital were my house keys and the empty packets of drugs along with the suicide note in a plastic bag, my dress had been cut off me apparently. Stewart and Kirsty encouraged me to speak to Mum and reassured me that she was OK and fairly intact emotionally. I finally plucked up the courage when she rang back for the third time that afternoon. She was amazing, I don't know how but she really was. Absolutely not what I expected her to be at all. She was calm, collected, level-headed and practical. I expected, worst case, her to be a broken, tearful, distraught mess, or best case, be angry and shout at me. But she did neither. I talked to both her and Dad; yes, we cried a lot, but they were both just so relieved to be speaking to their daughter finally and that I was alive. Mum was also now able to shed some light on my unanswered questions.

The police had managed to get my mum's mobile number off my phone to give to the hospital on the Thursday. The police I thought? How were they involved? Mum said, 'Your friend Sue called them to your apartment.' Now I was wondering, had Sue found me on the Thursday morning? Did she call the ambulance? But that couldn't be as I was brought in during the night. Mum informed me that 'Susan' had arrived at my flat on the Thursday morning and found it empty with my phone inside. She suspected something was amiss as I hadn't pitched up to the gym class I was booked on that morning. That's all my mum knew at this point, but she mentioned Mike my boss and Harvey one of the lads from work. And both Sue and Andy D had been calling her to keep her updated and support her. Sue had also read her the suicide note that she had found in the notes section on my phone. Poor Sue, poor Mum. I was still completely at a loss as to how I ended up at the hospital though and how the others were involved.

My older brother, Graham, was now also winging his way to my side from RAF Aldergrove and arrived first thing Saturday morning.

I was now ready to be allowed home as my heart had finally stabilised. When he arrived, we had clearly both had some time to process stuff. He walked in, again alone and just looked at me, eyes glazed over but in bewilderment and emotion. The rawness had worn off now and we were able to talk level-headedly about what had happened. Graham is an engineer in the army. He likes answers and solutions to problems. He was angry at the fact that the pharmacy had been able to issue all those drugs to me and wanted to get the absolute download from all the nursing staff about my recovery and how he could best help me. Sally my sister-in-law joined him, and we got ready to leave the hospital together as soon as I had been given a mental health assessment and they were sure I would not try to harm myself again. The mental health nurse seemed happy and signed my discharge paperwork, so I gathered my few belongings and Graham made me take a picture on his phone of the stack of empty pill packets as a stark reminder of what had happened. Brutal but essential, in hindsight. I asked if I could maybe walk home with them both rather than drive as it was only a five-minute saunter. You can see the hospital from my apartment, it's that close. Walking out of that glooming, dreary building and seeing the sky again and breathing fresh air hit me like a wave and I just stood and cried. We got back to my apartment where Kirsty and Stewart were waiting and called my mum and dad again to say I was safely home and surrounded by love.

Ten minutes later Sue knocked on the door. I opened it and we did not speak, we just hugged and cried. Sue's a boxer and probably the strongest, most tenacious woman I know. She has been an amazing best friend for years and I had just put her through hell. I looked at her and said, 'Please don't punch me,' to which we both laughed and went to sit on my bedside alone, while the rest were in the living room. Sue was the only person who had the full story, and more importantly my phone in her possession, which held many of the answers to the blanks.

She had arrived at our gym on the Thursday morning, and I wasn't there for the class I was booked on to. I rarely missed these and that week had pledged to her that I would try and get some proper routine back in my life to get me back on an even keel. She was looking through her Instagram, which she rarely does, while waiting for her trainer to arrive and saw the picture I had posted of my wrist tattoo 'Fear Not' along with the song *Arms of the Angels*. She put that together with my late-night message of thanks and instantly knew something was very, very wrong. She raced from the gym to my flat and in her words exclaimed she 'Didn't know her TT could go that fast'. On arrival, she got to my apartment door and thought it was locked. She called her friend who was a locksmith to come over to help her open it. She was now starting to get a grave feeling that something catastrophic had happened and in desperation pushed the door so hard it opened. Just at the same time, Harvey from Aerobility arrived at my building as well. He didn't know who Sue was so they had a brief introduction, but they both knew their mission. When I hadn't made the daily 10 a.m. Zoom call that Thursday morning Mike the boss said he had a 'spidey' sense something was wrong. Mike is in a wheelchair so sent Harvey round to check on me as none of the team could get hold of me despite lots of frantic calls and texts. Sue and Harvey came into the flat together and there was no sign of me and as they went around gingerly pushing open doors, Sue said she almost didn't want to push open the en-suite door in case she found the worst. On entering the living room, they saw some ECG strips on the carpet. This confirmed Sue's suspicions that something bad had happened. She found my phone on the bed but assumed it was locked so called the police to come and unlock it. She soon realised it wasn't locked and opened it to find a plethora of messages from concerned friends. The police then called back to say they had located me, and I was in HDU at the hospital. Sue then kicked into practical mode. She read through all the messages and found a message from Andy D who was very concerned and trying repeatedly to check I was OK. This name rang a bell and by now she had also found my suicide note draft that I had saved on my phone mentioning him. She decided to call him as she realised he was clearly a trusted friend. She also called my boss Mike to inform him of what she knew thus far. These three spent the next twenty-four hours supporting my mum down the phone and putting a recovery plan together for me. They were amazing. There was also a discussion between Sue and Andy regarding should they tell Skelfy. They agreed he deserved and needed to know, and Andy D called him as Sue wasn't too keen on discussing what had happened with him. The news was delivered that I had taken a massive overdose, was on life support in Basingstoke HDU and they didn't know why I had done it so maybe best not to make contact, in case he was a catalyst.

But I was still none the wiser as to how I was found, and neither was she. So, we looked through the calls made on my phone. On scrolling back through the many missed calls from colleagues at work and concerned close friends we saw that I had called the Samaritans' helpline at 0040 and the call lasted for thirteen seconds. I then seemingly had dialled 911 at 0050 and was on that call for eleven minutes. None of this I remember. And why the hell did I ring 911? Clearly, I'd been watching too many American films on Netflix during lockdown. Whoever was on the other end of that call was the voice that must have been telling me not to go to sleep I now realised. I was also told later by the medics that saved me that had my front door not been unlocked and if I hadn't have lived next to the hospital I most likely wouldn't have made it. I sent a letter to the crew a few weeks later, thanking them for saving my life that night. Covid had very nearly killed me but in a completely different way. I apologised for putting pressure on an already stretched NHS. My brain finally had clarity to realise just what a mess I had got myself into and how warped my decision-making had been. I know that now, but at the time it all seemed so logical. It was not a cry for help, it was mission to be completed. Thank God this time I was lacking in execution, or maybe there was another reason I survived.

I believe to this day that Anna was watching over me that night. I reckon I got up there to heaven and she said, 'Dude, what are you doing up here?' as was always her greeting to me. 'I am having way too much fun and you're not spoiling it yet. It's not your time, get your ass back down there.' I am utterly convinced she is my guardian angel, well at least when she's not cloud surfing up there as that was also her favourite pastime. I am so thankful that I did survive 13 August 2020. I have no intention of ever putting myself, my family, or my friends through that again. I will never ever give up on Liz McConaghy again. And I also want to try and make it clear to any person reading this who has lost a family member or loved one to suicide, it wasn't your fault. There is nothing you could have done to save them. I am in no doubt my family and close friends all asked themselves this question following my overdose and, thankfully, I'm in the lucky position to tell them, from my heart, that they couldn't have changed the outcome of that day. Once your brain has mentally checked out of life there is no way anyone can stop you. If you have made your decision, you will find a way. Even if Daniel Craig had called round for tea that night, I still would have done what I did. Suicide leaves a wake of questions behind it that people will never have the answers for. But hopefully now I have answered one for you. Could I have stopped them? No – you couldn't.

I'm not sure if Skelfy was a catalyst or not. But the week running up to the overdose, a mutual friend had posted some pictures of our little close-knit group of mates round at our old house where Skelfy had remained living after we separated. The photos showed them having a BBQ in the garden, on my old seats, holding my lizard and drinking out of my glasses, all of which I had left behind. It felt as if I had been cut and pasted out of my old life and it stung to see some of my mates that had chosen, for reasons I will never know, to shut down their friendships with me in favour of Skelfy. I will never

✂ DISCOVER MORE ABOUT PEN & SWORD BOOKS

Pen & Sword Books have over 4000 books currently available, our imprints include; Aviation, Naval, Military, Archaeology, Transport, Frontline, Seaforth and the Battleground series, and we cover all periods of history on land, sea and air.

Can we stay in touch? From time to time we'd like to send you our latest catalogues, promotions and special offers by post. If you would prefer not to receive these, please tick this box. ❑

We also think you'd enjoy some of the latest products and offers by post from our trusted partners: companies operating in the clothing, collectables, food & wine, gardening, gadgets & entertainment, health & beauty, household goods, and home interiors categories. If you would like to receive these by post, please tick this box. ❑

Mr/Mrs/Ms ....

Address. ....

Postcode. .... Email address...

Website: www.pen-and-sword.co.uk Email: enquiries@pen-and-sword.co.uk
Telephone: 01226 734555   Fax: 01226 734438
Stay in touch: facebook.com/penandswordbooks or follow us on Twitter @penswordbooks

Freepost Plus RTKE-RGRJ-KTTX
Pen & Sword Books Ltd
47 Church Street
BARNSLEY
S70 2AS

understand why people take sides without knowing the full facts in life, but it makes me sad, not angry, that, through my divorce, I not only lost a marriage but also some people who I thought cared about me – and of course half a family whom I miss very dearly.

Skelfy and I have bumped into one another since I came out of hospital. Many times, in fact, but he chooses not to speak to me, which I assume is a coping mechanism. What I do find heartbreaking is that neither him nor two of my best crewman mates, who I knew a long time before I met Skelfy, have ever been in contact to ask how I am or say that they are happy I survived. This will always be the saddest part of that chapter in my life. The collateral damage and finality that comes with divided love and loyalty.

Chapter 17

The Yellow Brick Road

I felt euphoric in the days after leaving hospital. I was able to discuss it with friends and put the whole episode down to the amitriptyline hijacking my brain. I looked at it as I had hit rock bottom and the only way was up. How wrong could I be? I was in denial. The truth was that all the amitriptyline had done was tiptoe into my brain and open the box where I had been storing many traumatic memories and experiences from over the years. It not only lifted the lid of the box, but it tipped the entire contents everywhere. The day after leaving hospital, I had to attend a mental health assessment in the local clinic. There were two lovely ladies who talked with me about what had happened and assessed my frame of mind. Basically, was I at risk of trying it again. They gave me a few leaflets about mental health and mindfulness along with a list of help lines to call. They directed me towards the Veterans Gateway helpline, circling it on one of the leaflets and assured me that Veterans Gateway would then get me on to their own system to start assessing my mental health for PTSD services and counselling. Before leaving, I asked the ladies when I would be seeing them again, to which the answer was I wouldn't be. No follow-up appointment, no phone call to check on me in a few weeks' time. This, I think was the most worrying lesson of all. Not only had I slipped through the healthcare net the day of my suicide, but as I walked out of their little room, with my polly pocket full of handouts about 'mindfulness', I thought, 'what's to stop me throwing this in the bin on the way to the shop to buy painkillers or a bottle of bleach?' Statistically, people who attempt suicide are most likely to reattempt within five days. Thankfully, I had a support network around me now with my brothers and their partners, along with Sue and close friends, who, understandably, were watching me like a hawk. But I thought about all those lonely and isolated individuals who may not. This is a huge flaw in how suicide attempts and mental health in general is managed in this country.

The mental health system in the UK is appalling, mostly due to lack of funding rather than the individuals who want to care for us, and it relies heavily on charities to take up the slack. I felt so lucky to have my friends and family to get me back on track but also to be a Veteran and have immediate access to support and not have to go on to some long waiting list. I made the call to the Veterans Gateway on that Monday morning. The hardest bit any Veteran or serving soldier with mental health issues will admit is making that first phone call. That's why Veterans Gateway have a number you can text for help as weirdly we all, myself included, seem to find that easier. I spoke to a caring, friendly Welsh chap who could not have made me feel more normal and was immediately referred to PTSD Resolutions and Help for Heroes. Just two weeks later I had my first counselling Zoom session. Unfortunately, I didn't click with my first counsellor from PTSD Resolutions at all, through no fault of hers I must add, but I would dread the sessions and leave feeling deflated and in tears. This is also a lesson I wish to pass on. If you do ever find yourself sitting in a room with a counsellor who is there to help you, but you just don't click, step out early. Like shoes, there are different fits for everyone. It is no slight on their ability but sometimes the connection just isn't there and when you need fixing, you must have the right glue, or you will just fall apart again. I realised during these sessions that there was no magic wand anyone could wave to fix me, and I thought I was broken beyond repair. I think for a time I went downhill rather than make progress. I finally accepted I may need to go on to some form of medication to at least get me on an even keel. I've always been so against taking medication, as I mentioned before, and the idea of accepting that I may need anti-depressants felt as though I was admitting defeat and that I was incapable of fixing myself. The GP, a much better one now, prescribed me a low dose of sertraline which is a very common anti-depressant to get started on. I asked her if I could only be prescribed two weeks' worth at a time as I was still so scared of where my mind could go, and I refused to have any large amounts of drugs in the apartment. Good job really, as I had another meltdown that November. I always find October into November a very difficult time. Anna died at the end of October and Roly also died in October so the end of that month running into Remembrance Day always hit me hard. And to top it off we were back in lockdown again, and now in the depths of winter. I went out walking the week running up to 11 November and thought to myself, I could just jump in front of one of these cars that were flying past me at high speed. I was still in such a dark place, but this time I recognised it. I phoned the doctor when I got home in floods of tears, and she upped my sertraline dose to 100mg.

Following that, I started my counselling sessions with Help for Heroes, I slowly became aware of the mountain I would have to climb to put these files back in some sort of order. There were many more dark days to come. I clicked with Pauline from Help for Heroes instantly though, maybe because that's my mum's name too. We could only have the sessions via Zoom calls due to Covid, but I would log on and within minutes the tap had been turned on and I was crying like a Tiny Tears doll. That was the difference, one set of counselling made me cry after I had left and this one made me cry while we were talking. That was the right way round I felt but maybe they both had a place. I cried and cried for months, finally letting go of all the tears I had stored up inside me over the years that I had never let leak out from my eyes in fear of displaying weakness.

I am not going to lie, I still struggled a lot over the next six months and my sertraline dose went up again twice over the winter of 2020–2021 until I was on 200mg, the highest dose they could give me.

When people say mental health is a battle, they are right. One day you are winning, the next for no reason at all you're not. The trick is to recognise those days and fight back. Remembrance Sunday always hits me hard and this year it did so more than ever. But now I had a huge support network around me to catch me when I tripped. They were there at every turn, checking in with me on social media, calling for random chats and popping by for a brew. Friends I had known for years and friends I had only known a year. Aerobility and Mike my boss were an enormous support. I have yet to have a Michael in my life that wasn't a huge influence or support in some way, my dad is Michael, or Mike, Grohly's middle name is Michael and Mike Miller Smith my boss, along with Mick Fry (Fryster) of course. Aerobility allowed me time and space to put my head back together without once making me feel like a burden when I had to down tools and just reset.

I was sitting in the office one afternoon and looked around me. Nearly all our employees had a disability, as do our flyers. I always thought I was the strong, able-bodied one. It turns out I was probably the most broken out of all of us. As what had happened to me became public knowledge it also opened a floodgate of messages in confidence from friends who had been through their own similar private battles. So many of us are carrying things within that we rarely talk about. I suspect everyone goes through something that secretly pulls them apart at some point in their lives. I was also lucky and had the best group of gal pals from Basingstoke who now took me out walking at every opportunity to help me offload to them and cry when I needed. They listened, they handed me tissues when I cried; they made me laugh. They noticed when I wasn't myself and dragged my sorry ass out the door or invaded my flat with biscuits and Prosecco so I couldn't spiral downwards when locked in alone again. I cannot stress enough how much getting some form of exercise can be beneficial to our mental well-being. Running had always been my coping mechanism but when I stopped during lockdown that's when my mental health deteriorated. And when you are in the grip of mental illness trying to get exercise is almost impossible as your brain just says, 'Not today'. It's a very vicious circle so I found myself having to force myself to get out into the fresh air for walks or drag myself to the gym, something that previously had been the highlight of my day.

I learnt through my counselling that when we are at war or in a traumatic situation our brains activate our frontal lobe, our fight or flight response. When this part of the brain is activated, it hijacks our reasoned thought part of the brain. Basically, over the years my brain had been trained to fight the enemy and remain alert, rather than run away as would have been a normal response. And because this response had been activated for so long it had begun to hijack my reasoned thought, hence the slow spiral out of control. It seemed perfectly normal to spend all day now in the flat, bingeing on sugar and not answering the phone to anyone. I knew deep down in my 'reasoned thought' this behaviour was bad for me, but that part of my brain had been overruled now. One of the observations I have made since my downfall is that mental health is very much taking centre stage and we, as a nation, are very aware how little men talk about their issues. It is widely thought that women are much better at discussing their problems openly with their girlfriends and family. But what about a woman surrounded by men. And what about a woman who is surrounded by men and whose husband is in the SAS and not particularly in touch with his emotions. I never opened up about any of my issues to anyone, I never cried at work in front of the lads, and I never wanted to be a burden. I just went further inward and became even more isolated. During lockdown, many people who had an inkling things weren't all quite right at my end would call me to check up on me. I would sit there and watch the phone ring and ring, not wanting to answer and having to put on the whole 'life is good' masquerade again. I am in no way a psychologist or a doctor, but I can now recognise these signs in both myself and others, and the only real way to start resolving the issue is to talk. To get it out there to anyone, a professional, a stranger via a helpline, a friend, or a family member – hell, even the man at the chip van! Do not do what I did and let it fester inside. If you can't bring yourself to talk and let it out then at least just tell someone that you are NOT OK, but you are also NOT ready to talk about it. That's enough sometimes just to make sure your friends are aware. Recognise the warning signs in both yourself and others if you can and reach out. If you see someone who you suspect is struggling and you ask if they are OK, ask twice. People will almost certainly say 'Yep I'm all good' or 'Living the dream' is a favourite military term, but if you ask again, 'Are you sure you are OK?' then that can sometimes prompt a vital reaction. If you are not OK, even though it's the hardest thing in the world, try and snap out of this robot-like response and say exactly how you feel. Give it a number. 'I'm a 6 outta 10 today bud' can sometimes be enough. I've learnt to be much more open with how I'm actually feeling now when asked and that in turn prompts others to open up as well as they no longer feel the need to pretend life is all good when it's sometimes not. We all need to steer away from this little dance of how amazing our lives are as we all know they aren't perfect 100 per cent of the time. We are real, we are human, we feel emotion and that is normal. We all have mental health, good and bad so share it. Certainly, don't try death, I can definitely not recommend it.

I finally finished my counselling with Help for Heroes in February 2021 and continued to remain afloat. But out of the blue I had my very first panic attack that summer. This was a horrible sensation and really knocked me for six. It happened at the gym one morning when I unexpectedly bumped into Skelfy. Panic attacks are horrendous; if you have ever experienced them, you will understand. It feels as though you cannot breathe. No matter how much you try, your lungs feel as if they are full of concrete, or someone is sitting on your chest. Thankfully, my bestie Sue was on hand to help calm me down and finally got me breathing again after finding me in a teary, hyperventilating mess on the floor in the spinning suite. I made a call back to Help for Heroes and ended up back in their hands for more counselling. This time my counsellor who had done her dissertation on anti-depressants suggested that sertraline wasn't the best option for me, and I should try citalopram. I begged the doctor for months to let me change and eventually in autumn 2021 they gave in and put me on to citalopram. It was a game changer. Within days I began to feel more like my old self again. My motivation returned and I didn't wake up every morning feeling as if I had been hit by a bus. Much the same as counsellors, with anti-depressants you need to find the right 'fit'. We are all different and our brains are all different. When things go wrong they all misfire differently, so the same drug cannot help everyone. I had been sticking with the sertraline, hoping that things would get better but deep down knowing it wasn't really helping. You know yourself better than anyone else does, so if you ever have a gut feeling, follow it, you will seldom be wrong. I'm far from out of the woods yet and although the citalopram is most definitely helping, and the dark days are fewer and far between, they sometimes still catch me out.

This year I was invited to go and march at the Cenotaph with the MERT and Medevac crews. Marching at the Cenotaph for Remembrance Sunday has always been a bucket list for me, and I felt so honoured to be asked. I would be walking with the team of angels who helped recover our soldiers along with many old Chinook friends and colleagues. I was telling everyone I knew that I would be going, then I didn't. On the days running up to the Sunday, I found myself becoming more and more anxious and couldn't understand why. I would be amongst friends remembering the fallen. My heart wanted to go so much but my head was pulling me in the opposite direction, and I began struggling to sleep all over again, debating my options in my mind. I reached out to an old friend for advice as I knew he suffered similar issues previously. He likened it to having an allergy to a food. Everyone else is eating it and you know you really want to as well but eating it will make you sick. This summed up exactly how I was feeling. He said, 'You don't need to be standing amongst thousands of people on Sunday to be able to remember those whom you hold in your heart, they will know you are thinking about them.' He was so right, and on making the decision not to go, instantly the breeze block on my chest lifted. These feelings of unexplained dread and doubt come to anyone with trauma, PTSD, or mental health issues. There have been many times over the last eighteen months when I have wanted to go to something so badly and had no reason to be fearful but at the last minute had a meltdown and pulled out. If you have a friend who is dealing with these issues, please go easy on them for always cancelling last minute. They certainly are not doing it deliberately and if anything, it is breaking their heart more than yours. That Sunday, I watched the parade on the BBC and wondered just how many Veterans felt the same as me. A national outpouring to acknowledge the price of war, yet many who came home are still paying that price and being imprisoned by their own wounds. I will never understand why the Cenotaph has the words 'The Glorious Dead' etched on it. There is nothing 'Glorious' about dying. The 'Glorious Unforgotten' or the 'Glorious Fallen' maybe, but that particular choice of words will never sit well with me.

Throughout my counselling, I learnt to accept the past traumas from my life but most importantly be nice to myself. I had become my own harshest critic over the years, saying things to myself that I would never have said to my worst enemy. I couldn't look in the mirror without hating what was staring back at me and I felt useless and lacking in purpose. I couldn't find the old Liz McC and was constantly searching my memories for her. I have now realised that much like a 'missing person', constantly searching for someone who has gone missing is very destructive. I finally realised that the old Liz McC was gone for good and there was an entirely new Liz McC staring back at me. I took time to mourn the old Liz and accept and embrace the new Liz McConaghy, who is a Veteran, a divorcee, a charity worker, and a suicide survivor, oh and of course a writer. I took all the best bits from my previous life and stitched them together to make a wonderfully diverse tapestry that makes me who I am today. Oh, and I fell in love again. With the girl in the mirror.

I am no hero, heroine or trail blazer. I'm just a crewman who put her thoughts down on paper to get them out of my head. The war inside will always be there, but I am on the stronger side now and hopefully I have the armour to keep winning from here on in. I have always said that your body can do amazing things providing you have control of your mind. I have finally got control of my brain once again, yes, folks I do indeed have one in there it seems. Some of the toughest battles of my career have been laid out over the pages of this book, but now I am facing the biggest fight yet and one that will last a lifetime. With all that I have learnt and my inner strength I know I can succeed, as I have a life full of love worth fighting for. My favourite film, since being a child, has always been *The Wizard of Oz*, and in fact I wore some bespoke 'ruby slipper' heels on my wedding day, with 'Wiz' written on the heels. Sitting here now reflecting on my journey, it feels as though I had been happily following the yellow brick road my entire life. Much like the fairy tale with the road stretched out ahead of me and all I had to do was walk along it. If you remember the film, Dorothy had to make her way through a dangerous poppy field to get to Oz, much like myself. But since 2017, those yellow bricks I was blindly following had been crumbling, and I eventually found myself standing in the middle of nowhere, with no idea how I got there and no yellow brick road to follow any more. I was looking around for the brave lion, the scarecrow with his brain and the tin man and his new heart. But none of them where there. Just me. Now when Dorothy gets to Oz the wizard tells her this vital thing: 'Dorothy my dear, you have always had the power inside you, you just didn't know it.' It finally dawned on me. I had my own courage, brain, and heart within myself. I could lay my own yellow brick road on a new path, anywhere I wanted to go. So, unlike most books, this is where my story does not end, it begins. I will lay my own yellow brick road and who knows what adventures it will take me on. When nothing is certain, anything is possible, right!?

And so, we come to the end of my book, not my story. I couldn't finish this without commenting on how I feel looking back and reading the pages I have written and how I now feel about our war in Afghanistan and the loss that came with it. I very much struggled to come to terms with the collective loss that I witnessed during my time on Op Herrick. If I'm truly honest with myself I knew we would never win that war, and I'm also not even sure what the definition of winning or success is when it comes to war? Can you put a price on a life? Can you add up the cost of war? We pay for it in love and it's true that there is no greater love than to lay down your life for a brother. Many ex-infantry guys I know said that being at war made them feel alive. They didn't fight for Queen and Country they fought for the man to the left and to the right of them. For me, I fought for the soldier in the ditch. That was my whole reason for getting airborne, the lowest common denominator.

Afghanistan will always win, and history has shown us that they have their own law and their own way of running their country. Who is to say that we should enforce our western blueprint of living on to them? In September 2021, America, twenty years after 9/11, withdrew their final military presence from Afghanistan. As the BBC reported each district falling back into Taliban control this feeling of 'what was the point' became all-consuming again. I watched Lash Kagar fall, then Kandahar and finally Kabul. My heart broke with each headline, remembering those fallen soldiers at each location who had paid the ultimate price and for what? Seeing the harrowing scenes of the Afghan people fleeing the country left me distraught, knowing what a horrible enemy they would come to face and the restrictions that would now be placed on their lives. They weren't fleeing for no reason; these people knew what was coming. The women knew that their lives would soon be over, despite being allowed to live. I knew these events were affecting many of my Veterans' mates, so I reached out and asked for their thoughts. The overwhelming response was this: if by us being there for fifteen years we bought freedom for one

171

child to grow up and have an education, we had won. If we bought the freedom for a child to enjoy flying kites around the streets with his friends, it was worth it. If we had allowed one female to find her voice, then we had achieved something.

I'm not sure what the future will hold for many of these women. I have been lucky enough to have a life that gave me the education and freedom to write this book, many of them will never have such luxuries. I reflect back on how I felt that morning when I woke up in a hospital bed and couldn't talk. There was a tube in my throat preventing me from speaking out and crying for help. These women in Afghanistan now have a similar restriction on their voices but there is very little they can do about it. I hope that if just one of them ever comes across this book it will be a message of hope and inspiration that you can beat the silent enemy, the darkness won't last forever, and you will find your voice again.

Here is a piece of work I wrote the week that Afghanistan fell back to the Taliban that sums up how I felt. Maybe someday I will find this little girl and write a book about her life as well …

The girl with no voice

Once, many years ago on MERT, my crew got a call to go and pick up a little Afghan girl that had swallowed a spring. Off we ran to spin the aircraft up, not really knowing how badly affected the little girl would be. Was she still breathing, was she even still alive? We made haste to get to her as fast as possible as was always the case on MERT tasks. On landing, I lowered the ramp and the combat medic raced off. When the dust cloud cleared from the rear of the aircraft, that we always generated on landing, I could see the medic talking with an Afghan man holding the hand of a little girl who clung to his leg. There were lots of hand gestures going on until finally all three made their way towards our ramp. I had put the toe ramps down to make it a little easier for the girl to walk into the aircraft, as without it she had to step up almost a quarter of her height.

As she came over the ramp, she looked petrified. I don't blame her. Children in the UK can be in awe of helicopters, yet they know what they are and what they do. To this little girl she had no idea what she was climbing on board and why. For all I know she thought we were an enemy taking her away to hurt her as we had a gun fitted to the ramp. Sadly, all Afghans, no matter how young, know what a weapon can do. I looked at her and gave her the biggest, warmest smile I could to put her at ease, but all I saw staring back at me were two beautiful wide eyes, big and crystal white, yet brimming with fear. My smile had no effect as she continued to cling to the man. As we got airborne, we found out from the medic that the man was her uncle and was accompanying her as he could speak a little English. She, however, couldn't speak any … in fact she couldn't speak.

The spring had lodged itself in her throat preventing her from being able to use her voice box. We got her back to Bastion swiftly and off she went into the British field hospital to be treated and have the spring removed. Now we very rarely follow up casualties we have rescued as it can be detrimental, for obvious reasons, but we decided as a crew to pay the little girl a visit the next day up in the hospital. We took with us some Haribo sweets and some tins of Coke from our aircrew rations to give to her. When we walked into the ward, I saw the same wide fearful eyes peering towards me. More people in uniform that she didn't recognise. Despite seeing her the day before we all had helmets on and I'm sure all her senses were so overwhelmed she would never have been able to recall our faces. Her uncle explained to her who we were. Still, she stared wide-eyed, not really understanding. So, we pulled the Haribo then a tin of Coke out of the bag we had brought. Her eyes instantly creased at the sides as she recognised the Coke tin. As we offered it to her the glaze of fear shattered into shimmering sparkle. She took it from our hands and quietly said 'Thank you.'

I look back now and think about her often. She couldn't have been more than 5 or 6 when this all happened. But that day the British Forces gave this little girl her voice back in more ways than one. I hope that she had the chance to use that voice throughout her life and learn new words and ways to express herself with that voice. I hope she used the words 'thank you' much more often than 'I'm scared'. I hope she had, for those twenty years, the freedom to use her voice. But most importantly I hope she still has that voice today and will continue to hold on to it wherever she is. I hope, no I pray, that another spring doesn't get lodged in her throat to silence her once again. For that little girl alone, it was all worth it. That little girl and her 'spring' of hope …

If you are suffering in any way with your own mental health don't wait like I did …

For Veterans:

Combat Stress 24/7: **0800 138 1619**
Or if calling is too difficult: Text **07537 173683**

For anyone and all:

Samaritans 24/7 Helpline: **116 123**

If you have enjoyed this book and would like to learn more or donate to the amazing Aerobility Charity then please visit **aerobility.com**

Index

INDEX